VOICESOFTHEPEOPLE

Joseph Bruchac

To all my friends in the new generations of Native artists and writers. Carry it onward. Wlipamkaani—Good Travels.
—JB

THANK YOU...

With much appreciation to Joanne Prince, Rainmaker Gallery in Bristol, United Kingdom, for all her time and assistance on this project.

ABENAKI SYMBOL KEY:

 — the supportive person in a family, a teacher

 — Thunderbird: a special helper of the Great Creator

 — self-pride or self-esteem for one's own heritage

Reycraft Books
55 Fifth Avenue
New York, NY 10003
Reycraftbooks.com

Reycraft Books is a trade imprint and trademark of Newmark Learning, LLC.

Text copyright © Joseph Bruchac

Art Director/Curator: Todd Kancar
Editor/Curator: Wiley Blevins (Associate Publisher)

Library of Congress Control Number: 2022906747

Hardcover ISBN: 978-1-4788-7516-1
Paperback ISBN: 978-1-4788-7515-4

Author photo: Courtesy of Eric Jenks

Manufactured in China 11292/19674/1122
11 10 9 8 7 6 5 4 3 2

First Edition published by Reycraft Books 2022.

Reycraft Books and Newmark Learning, LLC. support diversity, the First Amendment and celebrate the right to read.

Sonny Assu
Ligwiłda'xw of the Kwakwa̱ka̱'wakw Nations
Home Coming, 2014
Image: Courtesy of the artist and
Equinox Gallery (Vancouver) and Art Mur (Montreal)
Photo: Courtesy of the artist

INTRODUCTION

ABOUT THE ART

Cannupa Hanska Luger
Enrolled member of the Three Affiliated Tribes of Fort Berthold
and is of Mandan, Hidatsa, Arikara and Lakota descent
Future Ancestral Technologies: We Survive You
Image: Courtesy of the artist and Garth Greenan Gallery, 2021
Photo: Gabe Fermin

INTRODUCTION

Although there are more than 600 state and federally recognized Native American tribal nations in what is now called the United States, there is still a surprising lack of awareness about the history—or histories—of the indigenous peoples of America.

In recent years, thanks in large part to the work of Native American authors, the complexity and the importance of our cultures have become better known to the general public. It's better than when I was a young person more than half a century ago. Back then, the two predominant images of "Indians" were as Murdering Redskins or Noble Savages, and we were seen as a "Vanishing Race." Unless you wore an eagle feather headdress, rode a horse, hunted buffalo with a bow and arrow, and lived in a tipi, you didn't fit the popular stereotype of a real Indian—as it was molded by movies, television, and books by non-Native writers.

Even worse, the image of the "Indian woman" was that of a drudge, a slave to her husband, and a secondary figure at best. That is so far removed from the real places that indigenous women have always held. True, it varied from one tribal nation to the next and was impacted by the arrival of the Europeans with their own preconceptions about male dominance.

But, it can be said in general, women were at the center of every community, playing roles at least as important as those of the men. Among the Haudenosaunee (Iroquois) nations, the women were the heads of the families and clans, and chose the leaders in a society that was deeply matrilineal and matrilocal.

One of the stereotypes about our people that still persists is that our time was back then, not in the present—or the future. That is why the time frame of this book extends from pre-contact to the late 20th century. Native Americans are not locked in the past like fossilized insects in amber. We are here now and will be here in the years to come.

The thirty-four people whose lives I've chosen to represent in brief poems are only a few of the countless Native people of the past who should be better known. I've tried to offer a wide representation, both women and men, people who resisted as fighters, others who sought the path of peace. I've also limited my selection to those who have passed on at the time of my writing this and thus not included such contemporary figures just as worthy—such as the Anishinabe activist and writer Winona LaDuke or the eloquent Mohawk teacher and spiritual leader Tom Sakokwenionkwas Porter. Or dozens more who immediately come to mind. Their stories are still being written in their continuing work for all of us.

My hope is that this book may help its non-Native readers begin to gain a deeper understanding of who we were and who we still are through these brief stories taken from the lives of just a few of the historical figures we still remember and revere. I also hope even more that this book will be inspiring to indigenous young people—who also may not know these stories or need to be reminded that we have our own heroes.

Those you are about to meet are real people, not stereotypes. They are women and men who truly were, through their words and their deeds, voices of the people.

Left:
Jeffrey Gibson
Mississippi Band Choctaw/Cherokee
AMERICAN HISTORY, 2015

Artwork © Jeffrey Gibson, courtesy of Sikkema Jenkins & Co., New York;
KaviGupta Gallery, Chicago; Regen Projects, Los Angeles;
Stephen Friedman Gallery, London
Photo: Pete Mauney

ABOUT THE ART

    We have chosen to accompany each poem with artwork from a contemporary Native American artist. Some of these artists are members of the same nation as the person featured in the biographical poem. Their works illustrate contemporary concepts and concerns—many of which are the same as or similar to those of their ancestors. Other poems are accompanied by a Native American artist from another nation whose work connects to the subject of the biography in an important way. Our hope is that these works of art will expand the reader's view of Native American art and reveal how vibrant and significant it is in continuing and reflecting the hopes and struggles of Native Americans today.

Frank Buffalo Hyde
Onondaga Nation—Beaver Clan/Nez Perce
Buffalo Fields Forever—Bulls on parade, 2019
Image and photo: Courtesy of the artist

The Peacemaker

Wendat (Huron) circa 1000 A.D.

He came at a time
when the five sister nations
of Mohawk, Oneida,
Onondaga, Cayuga, and Seneca
were all fighting each other
engaged in seemingly endless
wars of attack and revenge,
an eye for an eye
and a life for a life.

He came in his
white stone canoe
across the waters
of the beautiful lake
bringing a message
simple and clear
that the only way
to survive was in peace.

Born among
the Wendat nation,
he came to them
because he said
the creator told him
that no one needed
more to learn
the ways of peace
than those constantly at war.

He told them that
if they continued
to follow those ways
of always fighting
the day would come
when there was no one left.

He showed them
how a single arrow
could be easily broken
but five tied together
would share each other's strength.

He combed the snakes
of evil thought from
the hair of Tadadaho,
the giant chief of the
Onondagas whose mind
until then was always on battle.

Then he planted
the great white pine
beneath whose roots
the war club was buried.

Seeing them finally
joined together,
he said I depart now
but remember always—
to hold onto peace
you must never let go
of each other's hands.

Rory Wakemup
Boise Forte Band of the Minnesota Chippewa
Darth Chief the Mascot Hunter
Image and photo: Courtesy of the artist

Jikonsahseh

Haudenosaunee (Iroquois) circa 1100 A.D.

When the Peacemaker began
to spread his message
of bringing peace where
there had been only war,
it is said that the one
he went to first
was the woman
named Jikonsahseh.

She had built her longhouse
along the trail
all the men took to war.
It was known that anyone
who wished to take shelter
there with her and get her advice
was always welcome
and in that time
of continual conflict
would be safe in her lodge.

So it was that people said
the path to war leads
through the house of peace.

As soon as she heard
the Peacemaker's words
it is said that she stood
and replied, "The words
you have spoken are good.
I embrace them and I
will walk by your side
as we try to lead
our people to peace."

Thus it was that Jikonsahseh
was there when the Great Peace
was finally made at Onondaga.
She it was who took the hand
of Atatarho, the powerful chief
who was the last to accept the peace
and helped make his mind straight.

In memory of the role she played
and in respect of the power
all women hold for peace
she became known
as the Mother of Nations.

To this day all the leaders
of the Longhouse Nations
are chosen by the women
of their clans who have also
the power to depose them.
When the men speak
they must always heed first
what the Clan Mothers,
the great-grandchildren
of Jikonsahseh, say.

Shan Goshorn
Easter Band Cherokee
Warrior Bloodline series "Wa-Hu-Wa-Pa" or
"Va-How-A-Pah" (Ear of Corn), Oglala
Wife of Lone Wolf
Image: Courtesy of the artist
Photo: Tom Pendergraft

Malintzin/La Malinche

(Nahua) circa 1500–1528

Was she a heroine
or a traitor?
One thing is certain,
that what Malinche did
meant she would never
be forgotten.
When Cortés and his
small army of Spaniards
arrived on her land,
she was given
to him as a slave.

Her Nahua people,
some say had suffered,
under the powerful rule
of the Aztecs.
So she was ready
to aid Cortés as
translator, advisor,
and one so trusted
she became his partner
in the conquest that brought
an end to an empire.

She also gave birth
to their son, Martin Cortés,
the first of that new race,
part European and part Native,
who would be called Mexicans.

The term malinchista,
traitor to the people,
was drawn from her name.
But there are those today
who see her strength,
her clever intelligence,
her will to survive
as an inspiration
and call her la madre,
the nation's first mother.

Jodie Herrera
Chicana and Indigenous (Apache and Comanche ancestry)
Jovanna, 2016
Image: Courtesy of the artist
Photo: Bruce Shortz/10,000 Crane Studio

Pocahontas

(Powhatan) circa 1586–1617

Pocahontas, which means
The Playful One,
was only her nickname.
Her name at birth was Matoaka,
The Flower between Two Streams
and, like that name, her life
became divided between shores.

All of the stories of romance
between her, a girl not
yet in her teenage years,
and Captain John Smith
were never true.
Smith's ritual adoption within
her Powhatan Nation
was the occasion that a
rough-edged Englishman
interpreted as a sacrifice
from which he was saved by
her tender heart,
when in fact, she was
only playing a part.

Taken as a captive
by those same English,
she always tried to help,
bringing them food,
even warning them
when their lives were in danger.
She was held as a hostage
for their own safety.

Finally released,
somehow she found a friend
and more in John Rolfe
whom she married—
their son Thomas a bridge
to connect two worlds,
or so she must have hoped.

We will never know
if the bitter wars
between her nation
and the English Planters
would have continued
had she lived
beyond her 22nd year.

For while in England
with her husband and child,
where she was revered
as a princess as she sought
support to start a school
back in Virginia to teach
Powhatan children the things
they would need to survive
in a world that was
no longer just their own,
she became ill, just as
their journey home began.

Taken back to shore,
she died at Gravesend
within sight of the sea
that divided her breath
from the land of her heart
and her dreams of peace.

Tony Tiger
Enrolled in the Sac and Fox Nation of Oklahoma
with Seminole and Muscogee lineage
Hope and Beauty, 2021
Image and photo: Courtesy of the artist

Tisquantum

(Patuxet) 1586–1622

Invited on board an English ship
then cast in irons and taken
across the seas to be sold
where he was sold as a slave,
he was freed from bondage
by Spanish monks,
then became a guide
for the Newfoundland Company.
When he crossed the ocean
he found his village gone,
most of his people killed
by some plague the English brought.
He truly knew then
what it was to be alone.

Yet when he saw
the white settlers struggling
to live in their settlement
built where his Patuxet stood,
he was the one who stepped forward
to help them, teach them how
to hunt, to grow corn,
served as their interpreter,
helped them trade with his cousins,
the Wampanoag nation.

Without his help
there's little doubt
the Plimoth colony
would have failed.

What did he hope to gain from this?
Was his dream to restore his village,
to live out his life in peace?
Would he have joined in Metacomet's war
that was fought less than a decade later
to try to drive back the white men
who had begun taking all of the land?

We'll never know, for his own death
of some unnamed disease
came just after the two first years
of the settlement where
the seeds were planted
that grew into the American nation.

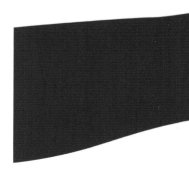

Gregg Deal
Pyramid Lake Paiute Tribe
Colonialism Spray Can
Image and photo: Courtesy of the artist

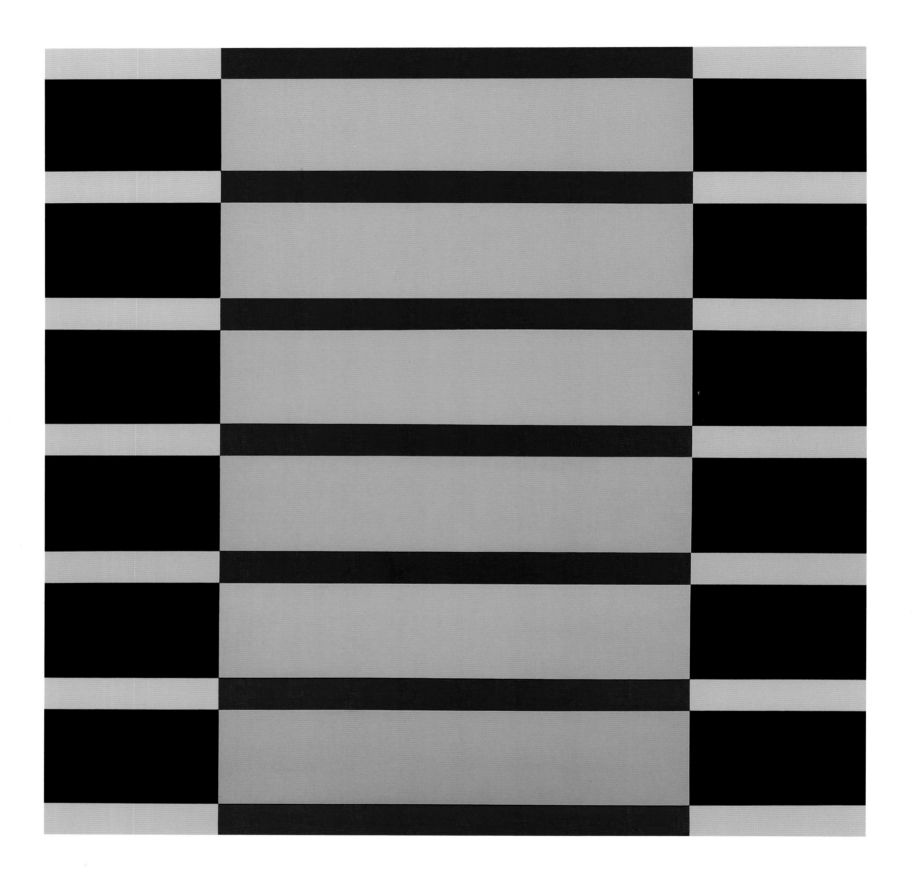

Jordan Ann Craig
Northern Cheyenne
She Wore Stripes; Sky Blue
Image: Courtesy of the artist
Photo: Jaida Grey Eagle

Po'pay

(Tewa) circa 1630–1688

Po'pay was a priest
among his people,
but the Spanish said
their beliefs were witchcraft.

He and 12 others
were brought to the plaza,
bound and whipped and kept captive,
until a crowd of the people came
and demanded their release.

That and the harsh rule
of the Spanish
were the reasons why
Po'pay planned their revolt.

Although they had never
worked together before,
this time all their many villages
and different tongues
found a common cause
and Po'pay led them in it.

Each village was sent
a knotted cord.
Untie one each day
Po'pay's message told them.
When the last is untied
on that morning
we shall all rise up.

The Pueblos did
as Po'pay asked.
And when the day
of the rising came
the Spanish could not
defeat them.
The beaten conquistadors
fled to the south.

It was many years
before the Spanish tried
to reclaim those lands.
By then Po'pay had passed on.
The villages were no longer united
and though many resisted
they could not
prevent the return
of Spanish rule.

But now, remembering
Po'pay's resistance,
the Spanish were
no longer so harsh.

In their kivas
undisturbed
the people continued
to hold onto their ways.

So it is why
more than four centuries later
because of Po'pay
and those brave men and women
who stood with him,
the Pueblos still stand strong
to this day.

Kateri Tekakwitha

(Mohawk) 1656–1680

Her Mohawk name meant
She Who Puts
All Things Before Her.

In her short life
the thing she put
before all other things
was her faith.

When she had lived
only four winters
her parents' lives
were burned away
by the smallpox
that left her own face
scarred and her eyesight poor.

Yet even with
weak outward vision,
what she saw for herself
was something deeper.

Her mother had embraced
the Catholic faith
and it was to that faith
that Kateri turned.

Despite her scarred face,
men sought to marry her.
But she accepted none of them.
She refused her aunt's order
to give a young man's mother
the gift of corn
that was a sign
she would accept him.

Instead, she fled
from the longhouse
to the Black Robes house
telling them her life
was meant to be one
of service and prayer.

She ate little,
but gave to others
offering her own suffering
as a gift to the Creator
asking the Great Mystery
to take pity on the needy.

She cared for children
and for those who were sick,
spent all her waking
hours in prayer
as she placed small wooden
crosses in the forest.
When she died,
her last words spoken
were "Jesus, Mary, I love you."
Chauchetiere, the French priest
who gave her last rites,
said that after her death,
all of the smallpox scars
disappeared from her face,
radiant with grace.

Venerated by those
of many nations,
her canonization finally came
more than three centuries later.

A bridge between
white and Native worlds,
she is known today as
Saint Kateri Tekakwitha,
the Lily of the Mohawks.

Alex Jacobs
Karoniaktahke
St. Regis Mohawk (Akwesasne)
ipod NDN, or Black Flint
Image and photo: Courtesy of the artist

Tom Harjo
Mvskoke, Lenape, Ogahpah, Shawnee
Wookie Water Warriors, Oceti Sakowin Camp,
Standing Rock Sioux Indian Reservation, 2016
Image and photo: Courtesy of the artist

Pontiac/Obwandiyag
("He Stops a Canoe Using a Spear Handle")

(Odawa) circa 1714–1769

Obwandiyag was a war chief
of the Odawa nation.

The French had been allies
of the Odawa, treating
them as brothers,
but at last the British
defeated them
after long years of war
and drove them from
the Odawa lands.

Pontiac then watched
how the British behaved.
He saw that they gave
his people no respect,
refusing even to sell them
the supplies
they needed to survive.
And though the British
had promised
to build no forts
in the Ohio country
it was not long before
they broke their word.

Pontiac stood up
and said this in council:
"It is important for us, my brothers,
that we drive from our lands
this nation which seeks
only to destroy us.
We must wait no longer."

So it was in 1763
that they declared war
on the British.

Other Native nations followed his lead,
Ojibwe, Potawatomi, Miami, Wea, Peoria,
Kickapoo, Mascouten and Plankashaw,
Lenape, Shawnee, Wyandot and Mingo,
in a wide alliance with many leaders.

It was Pontiac and his warriors
who destroyed Fort Sandusky,
won at Bloody Run, then
laid siege to Fort Detroit.
His was the spark
that lit the fire
for a war that
lasted three years.

It burned so strong
on that frontier
that when at last,
Pontiac met
with Sir William Johnson,
the British Superintendent
of Indian Affairs,
on July 25, 1766
at Fort Ontario
to end hostilities
the British made
this proclamation:
"All of the land west of the Appalachians
would forever belong to the Native people."

It was no fault
of Obwandiyag's
that this promise,
proved false,
but other tribal leaders
resented him for seeming
to take more authority
than he possessed.
So it was
that his death came
not from the British
but from the gun
of a Peoria assassin.

We have no true
image of his face,
though paintings
were made,
books and plays
were written
about him by men
who did not
know his story
and called his war
a conspiracy.

Few of his words
passed down to us.
But one thing
we know to be true—
he fought for
his people
and their land.

Samson Occum

(Mohegan) 1723–1792

Born a heathen in heathenism,
so he wrote of himself
in his autobiography,
the first-ever written
in English by an Indian.
As a child he was content
living the old way,
hunting and fishing,
not speaking the English
of those colonists
who took more
and more of their land.

But there was one white man
who came among them
to teach them their letters,
at the urging of
the Mohegan elders
who saw such knowledge
might help their people.

Like the other children he resisted.
Yet, somehow, he learned enough
to see the light
in the Christian way
was much like
their traditional ways
of trusting the good
and the guidance
of Mundu, the Great Mystery.

Four years he then spent
learning the Gospel
at the feet of the missionary
Eleazer Wheelock
who was his patron,
then went on
to become
a preacher,
and a teacher,
among the Montaukett people
of Long Island.

There he found a wife,
started a family.
Life was never easy,
for unlike other preachers,
because he was an Indian
he received only a fraction
of the support
any white man got.

Up before dawn
to hoe his corn, then
throughout the day
to travel among
the people preaching,
acting as judge,
doing all the things
to serve their bodies and souls,
sometimes going as much
as 30 miles on foot
to preach the Gospel
always receiving just
barely enough to clothe
and feed his family.

His preaching was so powerful
that Wheelock sent him to England,
there to preach and raise the money
that he was promised would be used
to support a school for Indian youth.

For more than a year
he preached across England,
confident that Wheelock
would keep his promise
and care for Occom's
wife and children
while he was gone.

He preached almost 400 sermons,
raised over 12,000 pounds—
an enormous sum for that time.
King George III, himself,
donated 200 pounds.

But when Occom returned,
he found his wife and children
nearly starving,
in rags
and living
in a broken-down hut.

And what of the money
he gave to Wheelock?
Not one cent went
to that Indian charity school.
Instead, the funds were used
to establish Dartmouth College,
a school for the education
of the children of English colonists.

Yet, Occom did not let
this betrayal discourage him.
He turned to help
other Christian Natives
form their own tribe
of "praying Indians"
and move to a new settlement
they named Brothertown
near Oneida Lake.

"I have endeavored,"
Occom wrote,
"to teach them as well
as I know how."

And so he did,
all of his life
remaining true to
his Indian brethren.

Greg Ballenger
Diné
Ouroboros
Image: Courtesy of the artist
Photo: Connor Ong

Ganio-Dai-Yo/Handsome Lake

(Seneca) 1735–1815

Although his people
had been loyal
to their friends, the British,
when the war was ended
the Americans ruled
and nearly all their land
was taken from
the once-great Seneca nation.

In despair, many men
turned to strong drink,
and Handsome Lake
was one of them.
His given name was that
of a Rodioner, one
of the fifty representatives
to the Great League of
Five Nations,
chosen by the women
of his clan
to represent them
with honor in council.
But alcohol made him
forget all of that.

He drank so much
that his body
failed him and he lay
so close to death,
his limbs grown cold
that his family thought
he had passed.
But when, like a miracle,
life returned to him,
he told everyone
of the great vision
given him by four messengers
from the Holder-up-of-the-Heavens.

They brought to him,
a new way to follow,
one that he must teach.

No longer drink the alcohol
that leads some men
to destroy their own lives
and sometimes even
kill their best friends.
Care for your families
and for the land.
Respect all women and
give love to your children.

In lesson after lesson
he related what he'd been given,
the Gai-wi-io, the Good Message
and the people listened.

And so it was
that Handsome Lake's vision
gave hope and new life
not just to him
but to the entire Seneca nation
helping to lead them
out of that time
when all had seemed
at an end.

CLYDE THE BIG RED INDIAN DECOLONISES TULSEY TOWN

Bobby C. Martin
Muscogee Creek
Clyde the Big Red Indian Decolonises Tulsey Town

Left:
Andy Everson
K'omoks and Kwakw̱aka̱'wakw
Resilience
Image and photo: Courtesy of the artist

Above:
Steven Paul Judd
Kiowa and Choctaw
Godzilla Helps Fight the Colonizers
Image and photo: Courtesy of the artist

Nancy Ward/Nanyehi

Aniyunwiya (Cherokee) circa 1738–1824

Nanyehi, "She Goes About,"
was Nancy Ward's Tsalagi name.
At Taliwa, in battle against the Creeks
when her husband fell, she leapt up
from behind a log, picked up his weapon,
and led the warriors to victory.
For that deed some also called her
by the name of War Woman.

But the title she was chosen to carry
because of her courage and her wisdom
was Ghigau, the Beloved Woman.
The head of the powerful Women's Council
and the only female voting member
of the great Cherokee general council,
she was the one to whom the leaders
of her nation turned for guidance.

In those times when everything her people
had cared for seemed about to be lost
she was a voice of peace and strength
spoken between them and the new settlers,
advising her people not to part with their lands
but also to take up such new ways
as weaving and raising dairy cattle.

In a letter she wrote to Washington
she asked the president for help.

"Our people would have more hoes, plows,
seeds, cotton carding, and looms for weaving.
They would learn your ways of cultivation. If you
send these things we would put them to good use."

When she was sent as an ambassador
to discuss the new American settlements
along the Little Pigeon River
she spoke these words to a white leader
who doubted that any woman
could do such important work:

"You know that women are looked upon
as nothing, but we are your mothers;
you are our sons. Our cry is for peace,
let it continue. This peace must last forever.
Let your women's sons be ours; our sons be yours.
Let your women hear our words."

Nanyehi, the Beloved Woman
whose words echo to this day.

Norman Akers
Osage Nation
The Okesa II, 2010
Image: Courtesy of the artist
Photo: Aaron Paden

Sacajawea

(Shoshone) 1768–?

Kidnapped as a young girl
by Arikara raiders
and taken from
her Shoshone people
who lived at the base
of those tall mountains
that block the way
to the western ocean,
she was taken down
the Missouri and Mississippi
to the villages of the Mandan.
There, still a teenager,
she became the wife
of the much older
French trader Charbonneau.

When the expedition led
by the two tall captains
came to those villages
they hired her husband,
not just as a guide,
but because his wife
was one of those
among the people
they knew that they
would have to contact
when the time came
that they would need horses.

By then she had a baby,
whose name was Pa-ump.
He became the darling
of the expedition
and Sacajawea
soon endeared herself
so much to everyone
that they called her Janey.

It's been said by some
that she was their guide,
but that was not till
they reached the familiar
lands of her people

far up the two great rivers.
Her true role, though,
was more important.
For wherever they went
the Native people saw
her and Pa-ump as a sign
this group of well-armed men
had not come to fight.
It was well known
to all tribal nations
that a war party
would never include
a woman and her baby.

Along the way,
her intelligence, her kindness,
quick wit, and gentle nature
endeared her to everyone.
And when the canoes
almost tipped over and
valuable papers and journals
began to float away,
Sacajawea was the only one
quick-witted enough
to grab them and
pull them back to safety.

Then, just as they
had planned and hoped,
when they reached
the Shoshone people
it turned out that
her own brother Cameahwait
was now the chief,
delighted to be reunited
with his sister and more
than ready to welcome
Lewis and Clark
and provide them horses
to complete their journey.

When after two years
that great expedition

was finally ended
she was invited
to the home of Clark
where she left her son—
who would grow up
to be a famous guide—
with the tall captain
to educate and care for
as if he was his own.

Some have written
that she did not live long
after that visit,
that she died of a fever
all because of the words
written in the journal
of one trader at a post
who said the Shoshone wife
of Charbonneau died there
of a fever, but did not
mention her name.

But old Charbonneau
had more than one
Indian wife and more than one
who was Shoshone.

According to Sacajawea's own
Shoshone nation
she returned to them
there near the mountains,
lived out a long life
known to all
as Woman Chief.

Her grave is still there
at Wind River Reservation,
beside the grave of her son,
her name carved into the stone—
Sacajawea, Woman Chief
the one whose legend will never die.

Chris Pappan
Kanza/Osage, Lakota
First People, Second City, 2014
Image and photo: Courtesy of the artist

Sequoyah

Ani-yun-wiya (Cherokee) circa 1770–1843

He was accused of witchcraft
for drawing strange shapes
on pieces of wood and bark
that some of his people
were sure were meant
to bring bad luck
or sickness to others.
His own first wife
and a band of others
waited until he'd left
their cabin filled with
those dangerous things—
then burned it to the ground.

But he had seen just how
the Ani-yonega, the white people,
used their own writing
to share their knowledge
and give themselves power,
and so he persevered.

Exiled to the west,
he continued to work
on his great invention,
until he had perfected
a way to write their Native
language with symbols
for each spoken syllable.

He returned, and with
his little daughter, Ayoka,
demonstrated how
he could write whatever
someone spoke to him
and even though she
stood far away,
when given his message
she could repeat it
word for word.

In less than a year,
nearly all the Ani-yun-wiya
were able to read
and write their own tongue.

And throughout the rest
of his long life,
Sequoyah served
as a leader, an ambassador
honored by his nation.

Jeff Edwards
Cherokee Nation
Cherokee On The Brain

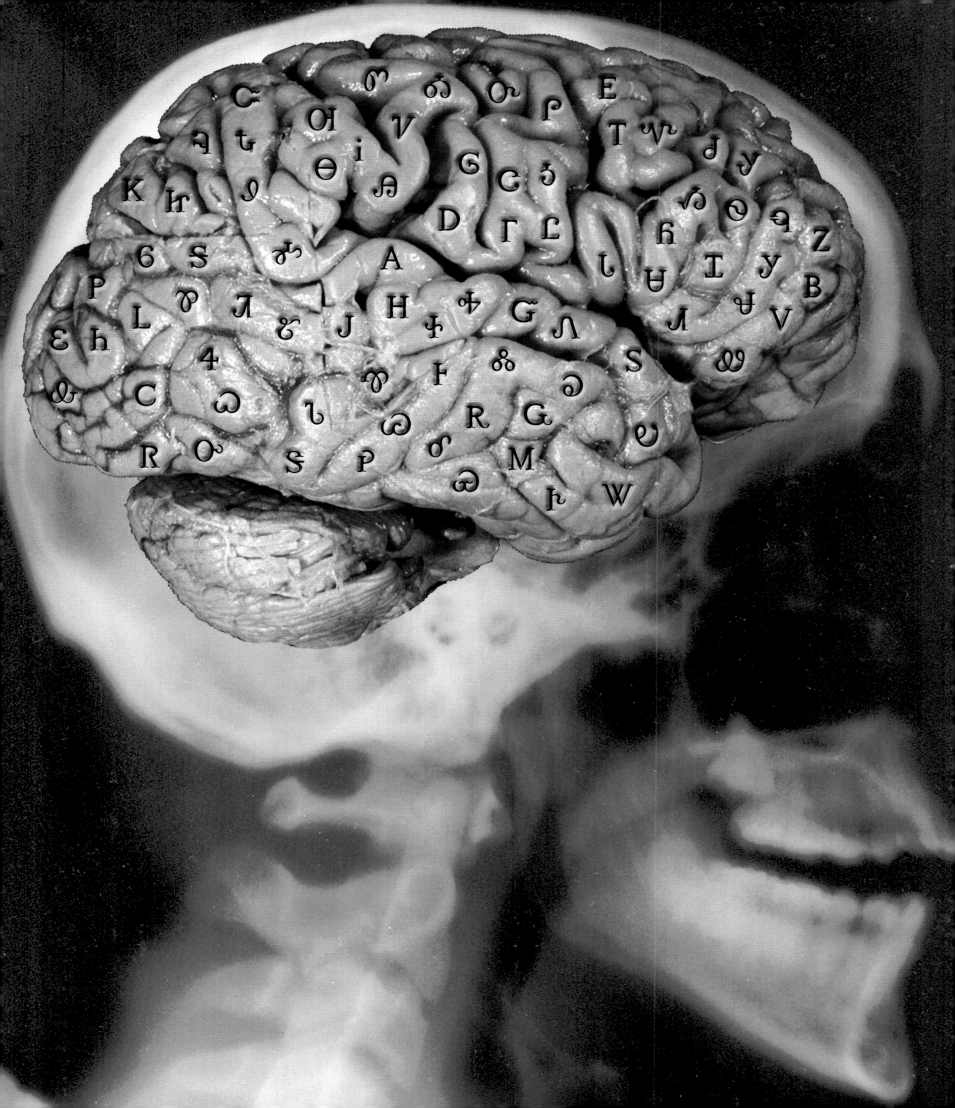

AN AMERICAN WARRIOR
WITH CLYDE THE BIG RED INDIAN.

Bobby C. Martin
Muscogee Creek
*An American Warrior
with Clyde the Big Red Indian*
Image and photo: Courtesy of the artist

Ely Parker Donehogawa

(Seneca) 1828–1895

The boy known as Ha-sa-no-an-da,
the Open Book, was chosen
by the Seneca elders
to defend his people,
by learning the laws
and the ways of the whites
whose hunger for Indian land
seemed to never end.

Given the name of Ely
by a missionary,
school was hard.

At first the twisted
English language
was too much for him.
He fainted while trying
to stand and translate
a sermon at the Baptist mission.
But he overcame
not just that obstacle
but every barrier
placed before him
till he could write English
and speak it not just as well
but better than almost
any other man.

Before he was born
it was said that his mother
had a dream in which
she saw a rainbow
arcing from their Indian land
to the great cities of the white men,
a rainbow broken
at its highest point.

Your son, she was told
by the dream speaker
will be a man great
in two worlds, going
from our land to theirs,
but always returning
to his own people.

And it was true
that again and again
he traveled to the cities
where power was held
seeking to prevent
the last of their land being taken.
Year after year
he argued their case
to governors and presidents
until at last
in the Supreme Court
their reservation was finally saved.

Soon after that
he was raised by his people
to the name of a chief
Donehogawa, guardian
of the great longhouse's
western door.

When he sought to study law,
his path was blocked
because no one
not a citizen
could become a lawyer
and no Indians
were citizens then.

But no law prevented
him from becoming an engineer
working for the federal government
designing and putting up buildings
that stand to this day.

It was while building
a customs house
in Galena, Illinois that he
became the loyal, lifetime friend
of the man named Ulysses Grant.

When the great war
between brothers began,
Donehogawa tried to enlist
and was told at first

no Indians
were needed
for this was a white man's war.

Yet when the call
to serve finally came,
he ended up
by the side of his friend.
As the best writer
in the Union Army,
Grant's personal secretary,
Ely S. Parker was the one
who wrote down the terms
of surrender.

And as General Robert E. Lee
shook his hand and said
"I am glad to see
one real American here,"
Ely Parker's reply was this:
"We are all Americans."

Geronimo/Goyathlay

(Bedonkohe Chiricahua) 1829–1909

No one on the frontier
was more feared
than the man they
called Geronimo.
His real name
was Goyathlay, the Yawner.

It is said the other name
came to him when
he and his warriors
won a great battle
against the Mexicans
on the day of
the feast of Saint Jerome.

Why was it that he
and his band fought
so fiercely against the white man?
They were not the ones
who began that long war.
When the Americans came
into the southwest
he and the other Apaches
offered to live
with them in peace.

But the Americans
took the side of the Mexicans—
those who had killed and
enslaved so many
that every Chiricahua family
had at least one relative
in servitude or working
in the terrible mines.

How many battles
did he fight,
always outnumbered?
From how many wounds
did he recover
over his long life?
Wounds not only to his body,
but to his heart
for more than once
he lost those he loved—
including his first wife
and children.

Feared by the whites,
even criticized by some
of his own nation
who felt that his resistance
put all of them in danger,
his true calling
was that of a healer.

He was known
for his medicine,
that he could ease
a woman's birthing,
heal wounds, cure
all kinds of sickness
better than almost any other.

The Sierra Madre,
those rugged mountains,
that he said loved him
were always his refuge.
No white man ever
could find him there.
His final surrender only came
when men of his own nation—
Chiricahuas used as scouts
by the American army—
led soldiers to his stronghold.

For their reward,
those Apache scouts
were loaded under guard
with all the others
of their nation onto trains
and sent to Fort Marion in Florida,
spending decades in exile.

In captivity, Geronimo
was exhibited at fairs,
brought out for the
inauguration of President Roosevelt.

He was never allowed
to return to the mountains
that he said "miss this old man."

He died in exile in Oklahoma
at Fort Sill, his grave still there,
placed on a military firing range.

Frank Buffalo Hyde
Onondaga Nation—Beaver Clan/Nez Perce
Virtual Sovereignty Study, 2021
Image and photo: Courtesy of the artist

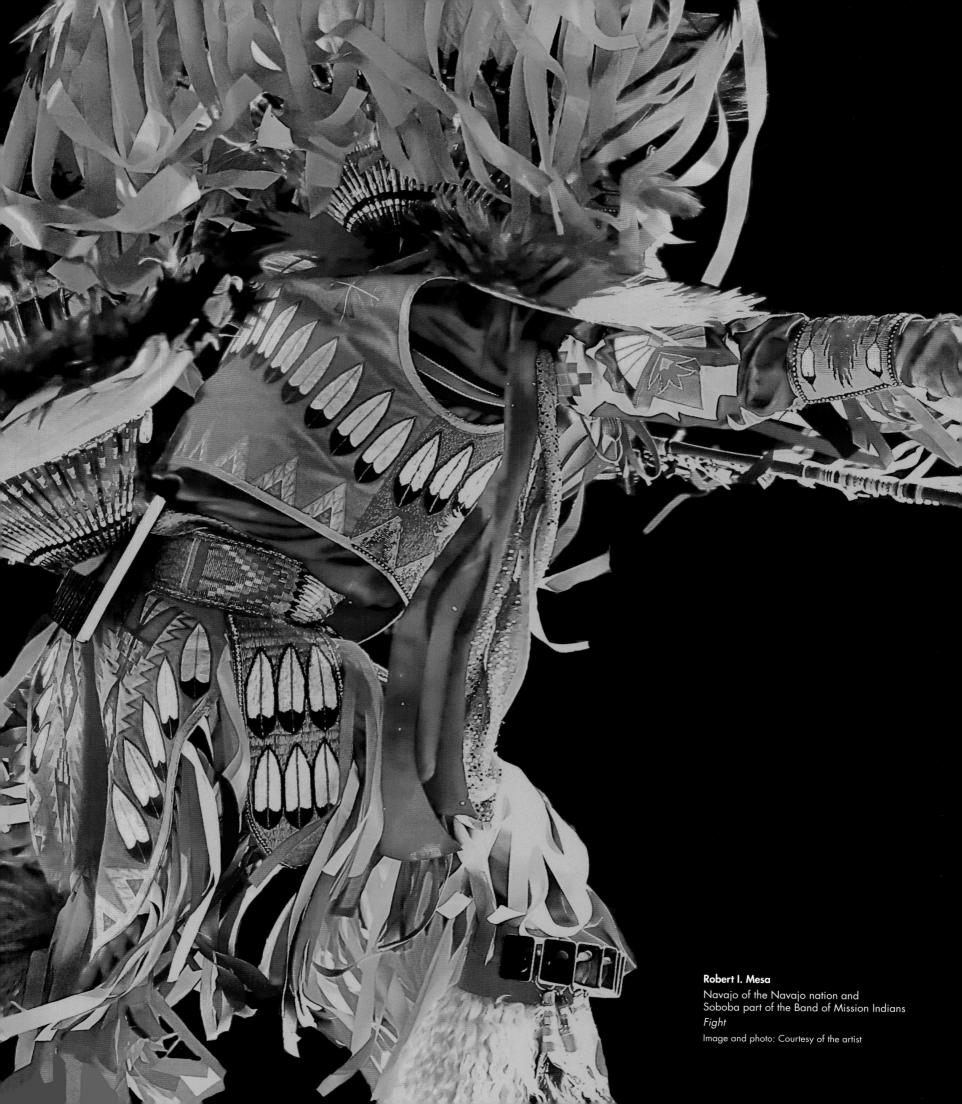

Robert I. Mesa
Navajo of the Navajo nation and
Soboba part of the Band of Mission Indians
Fight
Image and photo: Courtesy of the artist

Standing Bear/Ma-Chu-Na-Zhe

(Ponca) 1829–1908

In the Treaty of Fort Laramie
in 1868, the US government
gave the lands of the Ponca
in Nebraska to the Santee Sioux.

Removed to Indian territory
life was hard for the Ponca people.
Many died of starvation and malaria.
One of those who perished
was Standing Bear's oldest son.

In those days no Indian was a citizen.
In the eyes of the government,
at best they were little children,
at worst, beasts to be herded.

Standing Bear had promised
his son that he would bury him
in their sacred homelands
along the Niobrara River.

But when he left Indian territory,
carrying his son's remains,
he was arrested by General Crook
for leaving the reservation without permission.

His case was taken
to trial in Omaha.
There Standing Bear rose
and spoke these words:

"This hand is not
the same color of yours
but if I prick it
the blood will flow
and I shall feel pain.
The blood is of
the same color as yours.
God made me
and I am a man."

His words touched the minds
and the hearts of all those there,
including the judge
who made this decision:
An Indian is a person
under the law and entitled
to its rights and protection.

Unhindered then, Standing Bear
returned to their ancient land
by the Niobrara and buried
his son among their ancestors.

And when, three decades later,
Standing Bear, too, passed away
he was placed beside his son.

Today a statue of Standing Bear
stands proudly in the US Capitol,
the first Native American
granted civil rights under American law.

Sitting Bull/Ttanka Iyotake

(Hunkpapa Lakota—Sioux) circa 1831–1890

Many think of him as a warrior.
They remember him because
he was one of those
who stood against and defeated
Custer at the Battle of Little Bighorn.
But to his people
he was something else—
a leader who knew medicine
and always tried to heal
the wounds inflicted on them.

His name meant that like the buffalo,
he always faced into the storm
and could not be turned around.

When he traveled east
with Buffalo Bill's Wild West show,
a newspaper reporter asked him
why he was so respected
and loved by his people.
He replied by asking this question.
"Is it not true that among
your people a man is respected
if he owns many things?"

The reporter agreed that was true.
Then Sitting Bull responded.
"My people respect and honor me
because I keep nothing for myself.
Let us all put our minds together
and think what we can do for the children."

That is one of the things
Sitting Bull said. And his deeds
were always a match for his words.
While the Wild West show
was in New York City
he saw many white children
living homeless and hungry
on the streets with no one caring for them.
So, whenever he was paid,
he would walk the streets giving away
his money to those children.

Alex Jacobs
Karoniaktahke
St. Regis Mohawk (Akwesasne)
Homeland: Father at the River
Image and photo: Courtesy of the artist

Nocona Burgess
Comanche Nation
Mars Horse
Image and photo: Courtesy of the artist

Crazy Horse/Tashunka Witco

(Oglala Lakota—Sioux) circa 1840–1877

When he was a boy,
his nickname was Curly.
That was because his hair
was so much lighter and softer
than that of the other boys.

Sometimes, when white people
saw him with his parents,
they thought he was a captive,
taken from some European family.

But there was never any doubt
that Crazy Horse's heart was red.
He gained his name when he went
to seek a vision, all on his own,
without any help from his elders—
as always has been the custom.
He sat alone in an eagle catching pit
day after day, night after night waiting.

At last a vision came to him
of a man riding through a hailstorm
on a horse that moved with great power.
He knew that hail was actually bullets
and that the one who rode that way
would be him as a man, one whose medicine
was so strong he could not be touched in battle
as long as he always
thought first of his people.

His was the time when the Wasichus
tried to take his people from their land,
prevent them from following their old ways
of hunting the buffalo and living free.
So, he fought them again and again.

When he died, it was not from bullets
but from a bayonet stabbed into his back
by a white soldier after he had come
into the fort to speak of peace.
His last words were, "Tell the people
they can rely on Crazy Horse no longer."

His parents took his body into the Black Hills.
No one knows where he was buried.
But his spirit stays strong on Lakota land.

Buffalo Calf Road Woman

(Tsitsistas—Cheyenne) circa 1844–1879

The story of Buffalo Calf Road Woman
has been told and retold
throughout the years
by her People of the Striped Arrow,
the ones known also as Cheyennes.

The year was 1876
and the army of General Crook
was engaged in battle with
Lakota and Cheyenne warriors
led by Crazy Horse,
in what the Veho soldiers
called the Battle of the Rosebud.

Buffalo Calf Road Woman
was there, one who would never
let only the men
defend her people,
a woman as good
as any man with a rifle.

The battle was not
going well for them.
The white soldiers
were pushing forward.
Then, in the gully below her
she saw her brother
Chief Comes in Sight
fall as his horse was
shot out from beneath him.
Trapped by the soldiers
moving in on him
it seemed that he was lost.

But then, among the flying bullets,
she rode at full speed
down to his side,
pulled him up
onto her horse behind her,
and carried him to safety.

Taking heart at the sight
of her brave deed
the Lakotas and Cheyennes
rallied and fought
Crook's army
to a standstill.

It was not the only
courageous thing
this warrior woman did.
Her people relate that
she was the one
during the battle a few days later
with the 7th Cavalry
near the Little Big Horn River
who knocked Yellow Hair Custer
off his horse with a club.

But the deed for which
she is most remembered
is the one she did
that day by the Rosebud,
that battle described
by all her people as
The Fight Where
the Girl Saved Her Brother.

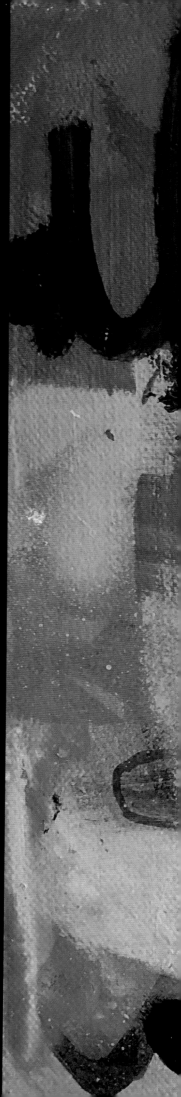

George Alexander
Muscogee
Jingle Grafitti
Image: Courtesy of Jo at Rainmaker Gallery
Photo: Patricia Pantlin

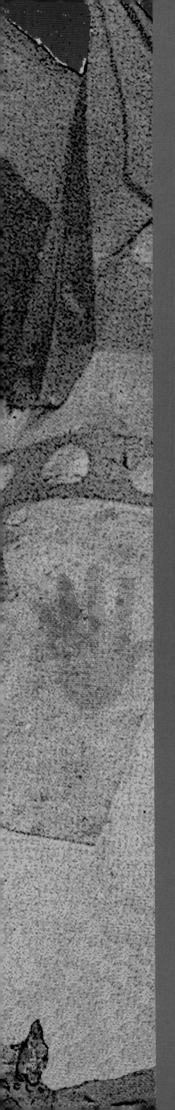

Quanah Parker

(Comanche) 1845–1911

His mother's name
was Cynthia Parker
before she was captured
at the age of nine,
given the name of Nadua
and adopted into
the Nokoni band
of Comanches.
Wedded to Peta Nocona,
a warrior chief, they
had three children
and her first child
was Quanah,
who grew himself
to be a war leader
among the Antelope Eaters,
the Quahadi Comanche band.

His mother never
wished to return
to the life she'd left behind.
Taken by the Texas Rangers
with her daughter Topsannah,
and returned to her white family,
neither she nor her daughter
lived much longer.
Her daughter died of a fever
and Nokua, who was
no longer Cynthia,
refused to eat and starved.

When, in 1874,
Quanah's people joined forces
with the Kiowa and
the southern Cheyenne
to try to drive out
the buffalo hunters
who were destroying
their way of life,
he led them in battle
until their village

in the Palo Duro Canyon
was destroyed
and all of their beloved horses,
more than a thousand,
were killed by the Army.

Impoverished,
with no provisions,
Quanah's Quahadis
were the last
of the tribes
of the southern plains
to surrender in 1875.

Had his story ended there
it would not have been different
from that of so many others
who tried to resist
the Long Knives and lost.

But Quanah was never
like other men.
On the reservation
he reached out
to his mother's relatives,
went to visit them, learned English,
studied western ways,
including cattle ranching
and from then on
called himself
Quanah Parker.
Named by the government
to be the chief of
all the Comanches,
he became a prosperous rancher,
helping his people and
respected by his white neighbors
in Oklahoma.

When he was
gored by a bull

while visiting his white relatives,
he lay near death
until a curandera,
a Mexican medicine woman,
gave him a peyote tea,
a natural antibiotic
that healed him
and he went on to live
to the age of 66.

After his recovery,
he began to teach
the sacrament of peyote,
became a founder of
what would become
the Native American Church,
now found in nearly
every Native tribal nation.

The white man, Quanah said,
goes into his church house
and talks about Jesus.
But the Indian
goes into his tipi
and talks with Jesus.

Buried in Fort Sill,
near the graves
of his mother and sister,
on his stone these words
are engraved:

Resting Here Until Day Breaks
and Shadows Fall and Darkness
Disappears Is
Quanah Parker
Last Chief of the Comanches.

Debra Yepa-Pappan
Jemez Pueblo and Korean
Hello Kitti Tipi, 2006
Image and photo: Courtesy of the artist

Chief Joseph/In-Mut-Too-Yah-Lat-Lat

(Nez Perce) 1840–1904

"What I have to say
will come from my heart,
and I will speak
with a straight tongue.
Ah-cum-kin-i-ma-me-hut,
The Great Spirit,
is looking at me
and will hear me."

So the Nez Perce chief
In-mut-too-yah-lat-lat,
Thunder Traveling Over the Mountains,
the one known to white men
as Chief Joseph, began
as he told the story
of his people and the war
they were forced to fight.

Since their first meeting in 1805
with the starving white men
led by Lewis and Clark
to whom they said
"We are poor but our hearts are good"
as they fed them and treated them
with great kindness,
it had been the pride
of the Nez Perce people
that they were friends
with the white men.

"Our fathers gave us
many laws," he said.
"They told us to treat all men
as they treated us, that we
should never be
the first to break a bargain."

But that was not
the way his people
were treated,
as more and more
white men came
to settle on their lands
and at last they were told,
though they gave up
much of their land,
to leave their homes
and go to a small reservation
leaving the graves
of their fathers behind.
They had tried hard
to live quietly,

despite the fact
that the white men
who now were all around them
would not leave them alone,
stealing their horses,
branding their young cattle,
insulting them.
Finally some of Joseph's people
could stand it no longer.
Led by one whose father
had been killed
by a white man who went unpunished,
a group of young Nez Perce men
went out and killed four white men.
That was when Chief Joseph
saw there was no way
to avoid a war, though
they still tried to escape fighting,
gathering their people
in a camp at White Bird Creek,
getting ready to leave
for the Buffalo Country.
That was where the first army
attacked them,
and where the white soldiers
learned to their dismay
that when they were
finally forced into battle
the Nez Perce were fierce.
"When an Indian fights,"
Joseph explained,
"he only shoots to kill,
but soldiers shoot at random."

In that brief battle,
which ended with the army
in panicked flight,
the Nez Perce numbered
only sixty men, and the soldiers
more than a hundred.

One after another,
as they retreated,
Chief Joseph's always
outnumbered people,
never more than
three hundred fighting men,
met one army after another,
outmaneuvering and defeating
the forces of General Howard,
General Gibbon, and General Sturgis,
still hoping to reach

the Buffalo Country
across the border in King George's land
where Sitting Bull and his Lakotas
had gone after the battle
of the Greasy Grass where they
defeated Custer.

Finally the army
of General Miles
met them at Bear Paw Mountain,
stood between them
and Sitting Bull's nearby camp.
Had they left their wounded,
old women and children, behind
they could have escaped.
But, as Chief Joseph said,
"We were unwilling to do so.
We had never heard
of a wounded Indian recovering
while in the hands of white men."

And so, as he gave up his gun
to General Miles, he spoke these words
"From where the sun now stands,
I will fight no more forever."
When Chief Joseph ended
his talk in Washington,
two years after the war,
he pleaded that his people
who were dying in exile
might be allowed
to finally return to their lands.

"I ask only,
to ask of the government
to be treated as all
other men are treated,"
Chief Joseph said,
his voice as deep
as thunder across the mountains.

"Then the Great Spirit Chief
who rules above
will smile on this land
and send rain
to wash out the bloody spots
made by brothers' hands
upon the face of the earth."

Frank Buffalo Hyde
Onondaga Nation—Beaver Clan/Nez Perce
Virtual Sovereignty #2, 2021
Image and photo: Courtesy of the artist

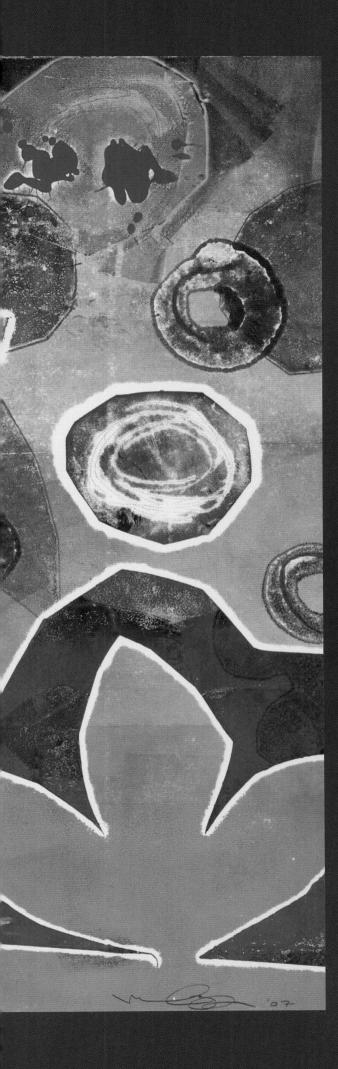

Lozen

(Chiricahua) 1845–1899

With good reason
they called her
a warrior woman.

Sister of the great
Chief Victorio, she fought
beside Geronimo
in their long battle
to keep
their Chiricahua lands.

It is said that
she never
showed any fear,
even when
the enemy was near.

When the Long Knife soldiers
attacked their village
in the White Mountain
where they were now
trying to live in peace,
it was Lozen who circled
behind the soldiers
and drove off
their horse herd.

Although her courage
was equal to
or more than that
of any man,
fearlessness was not
her only strength.

She had been given
a gift of power,
the power to know
where enemies were.

She only had
to hold up her hands
and feel the warmth
that came to them
to know the direction
of those soldiers
who could never
catch her band.

If it was not for
Chiricahua scouts,
who chose to help
the Americans,
she and her defiant
brothers in arms
never would
have been found.

She took
no husband,
had no children.
Her nation
was her family.

And with all of them,
their entire tribe—
even those scouts
who'd worn uniforms—
Lozen was sent
into exile
in a bitter prison
camp in Alabama
where she died.

But although her body
never returned
to those beloved
mountains she defended,
her spirit remains
there in those canyons
of Arizona and old Mexico,
uncatchable and
forever free,
reminding her people
to never give in.

Melanie Yazzie
Diné (Navajo)
From the Woods, 2007
Image: Courtesy of the artist
Photo: Margot Geist,
University of New Mexico Art Museum

Sarah Winnemucca/Thocmetony

(Paiute) circa 1855–1891

The name she was given
as a child was Thocmetony,
which means Shell Flower
and, though small,
she seemed as lovely
as a blossom.

But her life and those
of all her people
were hard in those days
when they feared the Taibos,
the dangerous white men
who were ready to shoot
any Indian they saw.
The Paiutes believed then
that those Taibos were cannibals.
All of the Native people
of the Sierras knew the story
of the party of settlers
caught in winter snow,
who consumed the dead bodies
of their own people
after killing and eating
their Indian guides.

One day when
Thocmetony was very small
her mother and her aunt
heard white men were near
and fled in panic, carrying
her and her cousin
until they were too tired
to carry them any further.
So they buried her and her cousin
in the sand up to their necks
with bushes placed
over their faces to hide them.

But, as she grew older,
now known as Sarah—
her last name that
of Winnemucca, her father—
she began to learn
English and Spanish
from a settler family
who hired her and her sister
to do chores and care
for their own small daughter.

Though she spent a brief time
in a Catholic school,
Sarah mostly taught herself
to become so fluent in
reading and writing

she was asked
by a sympathetic
army officer
to write letters about the state
of her people, who
had been confined
to a small reservation,
badly treated and starving.

Her beloved grandfather
known as Captain Truckee
had taught that their lives
would be better
if they followed more
of the white people's ways.
And throughout her life,
like Truckee, Sarah believed
all could live together,
both Indian and white.

She was hired then
by the US Army
to be a translator during
the war that was fought
against their cousins,
the Bannock nation.
No other interpreter
could speak not only
fluent English and Spanish,
but also Paiute, Bannock,
Washoe, and other Native tongues.
She acted as a messenger,
a translator, and a mediator
teaching the English language
to Native children and
the Indian prisoners.

After that war,
she began to travel,
with the help of two
remarkable sisters,
strong advocates of
Native and women's rights:
Elizabeth Peabody
and Mary Peabody Mann.

Appearing on hundreds
of eastern stages,
colorfully dressed
and advertised as
the Paiute Princess
she spoke of
the struggles of her people,
about the rights denied to them

Her eloquence, her humor,
and her storytelling
earning standing ovations
as she cried again and again
"It Can Be Done!"

While Sarah
was in Boston,
at Mary's suggestion
she began work
on a book that would
incorporate and expand
on her eloquent lectures.
And so it was that
in 1883, her book
Life Among the Piutes,
Their Wrongs and Claims
was published.
The first book ever written
by a Native woman
of the west,
it was widely acclaimed.

But her criticism
of the reservation system
and its corrupt Indian agents
earned her many enemies
and when she returned
to the west, she found
no one would ever hire her
again as an interpreter.

Undaunted,
two years later
in Lovelock, Nevada,
she started her own school.
Unlike the government's
boarding schools,
she encouraged both
English and Native languages,
celebrating cultural traditions,
not trying to erase
all that was Indian.
In a letter she wrote
to Paiute families, she said
what she wished to do
was to "fit your little ones
for the battle of life,
so that they can attend
to their own affairs
instead of having
to call on a white man."

Her school was far
ahead of its time.
Reservation officials
opposed it,
sometimes coming
and taking away
the children by force.
In 1889, Sarah was forced
to close her school.

Money was short
and Paiute parents
were withdrawing their children
because they believed
in the Ghost Dance,
taught by Wovoka,
the Paiute prophet
who promised them
the old ways would return
if they gave up all Taibo ways,
including speaking English.

Discouraged and
not in good health,
it still seemed as if
Sarah had many
years ahead of her.
But on October 16, 1891,
at the age of 47,
she died suddenly
from unexplained causes.
Some suspect that
she was poisoned
by one of her many enemies.

The life of Sarah Winnemucca
the Paiute Princess ended,
but her legacy continues.
Her vision of education
for Native children
that includes our languages
and customs while
equipping our children
to succeed in the wider world
has become the norm
in our community schools.

Yes, it could be done.

Shelley Niro
Bay of Quinte Mohawk
Legacy
Image and photo: Courtesy of the artist

Wovoka

(Paiute) 1856–1932

The white rancher
he worked for
knew him as Jack Wilson,
a gentle man,
little different from
any other Paiute
farmhand in
that dry land.

Almost always quiet
and unassuming.
in his tall black hat,
he hardly would
have stood out
in a crowd
until he spoke.

He spoke of how
his great vision
showed him what
his people needed
to know.

If they would
just gather,
hold hands
in a circle,
sing and dance
together,
the land would roll up
and then
when it unrolled
all those
who hurt them
would be gone
and the buffalo
would return.

There would be
no need for violence,
for the Great Spirit
would take pity
upon them
and make this
come to be.

His vision was
so powerful
that it crossed the land
to other tribal nations—

suffering, like his
from the loss
of all that made
their lives good.

So they, too,
began to dance.

Seeing the Indians
gather together,
the US government
became afraid.

They had heard
that the Lakotas,
those great warriors,
believed if they wore
a special thing
called a ghost shirt
no bullets could
ever touch them.

And, when a group
of those Lakotas
left the reservation
to go and dance,
the army pursued
and encircled them
as they stood
offering no resistance.

Then a shot was fired
and the army's big guns
opened fire
and hundreds
of Lakota people died
at that place
called Wounded Knee.

Wovoka heard
of that massacre.
That day he bowed
his head in sorrow—
a sorrow that stayed
with him all of his days
as he mourned
the failure of
a beautiful dream.

Chris Pappan
Kanza/Osage, Lakota
Eagles Shadow
Image and photo: Courtesy of the artist

Charles Alexander Eastman/Ohiyesa

(Santee Dakota) 1858–1939

In his book,
An Indian Boyhood,
he told of how
he learned the ways
of his Santee Dakota people
from his grandparents
in the absence of his father,
how he gained the name
of Ohiyesa and lived
a life that he believed
every boy would dream
of living, never mentioning
how his entire nation
was driven out
of their homelands,
how when they rose up
they were punished,

how the mass hanging
of the leaders
of their rebellion
was the largest
in all of US history.

After gaining
an eastern education,
he devoted his life
to healing—
both as a doctor
and as an author.
In all his books
he wrote about
the way his Native people
followed a path
of spirit and balance,

one that he believed
all the world
would do well to follow.

He held out hope,
even though he
he had seen the worst
done to his people.
After the terrible massacre
of Chief Bigfoot's peaceful
Lakota ghost dancers
by the seventh cavalry,
while he was the doctor
at Pine Ridge reservation,
he was the first one
who ventured out
into the snows

to try to rescue
any who had survived.

One of the founders
of the Boy Scouts
of America,
throughout his life,
he dreamed
of a path that
all might follow,
no matter their nation,
a path that far
too few have
chosen to walk.

Susan La Flesche

(Omaha) 1865–1915

Her father's name was Iron Eye
and her own gaze was just as steely.
The youngest of five children,
the Omaha language
was the only one
that was spoken in her family.

Born on the Omaha reservation
one thing that happened
when she was a child
may have showed her
the path that she would follow—
when she saw
a sick Omaha woman die
when a white doctor
refused to treat her.

After her years at the boarding school
where Native children were taught
to forget all that was Indian,
she went on to study
at schools in the east,
including Hampton College,
a Black school
where Native Americans
were welcomed.

On her graduation,
instead of following
the path that many
urged her to follow—
return to her reservation
and teach or just
become a good
Christian wife and mother—
she chose to become a physician
and was accepted at the
Women's Medical College
of Pennsylvania,
graduating three years later
as the valedictorian.

As the first Native
American woman
to become a doctor
her eyes remained
fixed on one goal.

At last she could
help her people.
And so, she returned
to her Omaha reservation
as a medical missionary.
There she fought
the curse of alcohol
that destroyed the health
of so many and was used
by white men to convince
drunk Omahas to sell their land.

She brought the first
private hospital to
any Indian reservation,
crusaded against the tuberculosis
that would take the life
of the man she married,
and traveled again and again
to Washington trying
to protect Omaha land
and prove that Indians
were not children,
but citizens deserving
the chance to find
their own paths to follow.

Her picture of a future
in which her people
might enjoy good health
and hold on
to their ancestral lands
never faded.
For more than
a quarter of a century
she served them
until her own passing,
leaving behind
her undimmed vision
of a brighter future
to be seen through
the eyes of the next
Omaha generations.

Marie Watt
Member of the Seneca Nation of Indians
and also has German–Scot ancestry
Companian Species (Fortress), 2017
Image: Courtesy of PDX Contemporary Art and the artist
Photo: Aaron Johanson

Elizabeth Burton "Lyda" Conley

(Wyandot) 1869–1946

Lyda Conley was the first woman
admitted to the Kansas bar,
in 1900—a time where
there were few other women lawyers,
much less one of Native descent.

Lyda was proud
of her Wyandot ancestry,
even though in 1855
her people had accepted
an offer of US citizenship
and the division of their land.
Other Wyandots had not
agreed and went to Oklahoma,
though they kept authority
over the tribal burying grounds,
the Huron Indian Cemetery
there in Kansas City,
where Lyda's family lived.

Then, in 1906 the Wyandots
of Oklahoma approved the sale
of that Huron Indian Cemetery—
the graves to be removed,
the land opened for development.

But it was the place
where Lyda's ancestors
and many other Wyandot people
had been buried.

Lyda and her two sisters
would not stand for it.
They built a small shed
inside the burial ground
and moved in to protect it
around the clock,
put up No Trespassing signs,
and took turns
standing guard with muskets.

Lyda's words were recorded
in the Kansas City Times:
"Why should we not be
proud of our ancestors
and protect their graves?
We shall do it, and woe be
to the man who first attempts
to steal a body!"

She filed a petition
in the US circuit court
for an injunction
against the sale.
When that court ruled against her,
she took her case on appeal
to the Supreme Court
of the United States.

There she pled their case,
the first female Native American
admitted before the court.

Though they ruled against her,
Lyda and her sisters continued
to protect the burying ground.
They gained so much attention
that Senator Curtis of Kansas,
himself of Native ancestry,
introduced a bill to Congress
that made the land a national park
when it was passed in 1916.

Through the years that followed,
Lyda continued to practice law
and watch over that land.
She brought food and water
to the birds and squirrels
that lived there and guarded
the sacred burial place
until her death 30 years later.

Lyda and her sister Elena
lie side by side
in that cemetery,
close to the bones
of their ancestors forever.

WYANDOTTE NATIONAL BURIAL GROUND
Cursed Be the Villain That Molest Their Grave
is the inscription on her sister's stone.

Gertrude Simmons/Zitkala-Sa

(Yankton Dakota) 1876–1938

Daughter of
a Yankton Sioux mother
and white father,
known then as Gertrude Simmons
she was brought up
in the Lakota way
until at the age of eight
she was sent away
to the Indiana Manual Labor Institute.

There her long hair was cut
and everything was done
to strip from the stubborn girl
all that was Indian,
but they did not succeed.

In her teens she changed her
name to Zitkala-Sa,
which means Red Bird.
And like that bird
she began to fly,
first to Earlham University
and then to study music
at the New England Conservatory,
and become a teacher.

She had learned from her mother,
Tate Iyohiwin,
Reaches For the Wind,
that the voices of women
were meant to be heard.
And so it was that
she began to write
about the struggle
to stay true to one's culture
in a world that seldom listened.

Her essays and books
became widely read
and the opera,
The Sun Dance Opera,
for which she
wrote the libretto and
contributed the Lakota songs
she played on her violin,
was the first by
any American Indian.

Co-founder of
the National Council
of American Indians
and its president
for the rest of her life,
she led the fight
for all Native people's rights
for health care and education,
for citizenship, and the respect
truly owed to them.
There can be no doubt
that Zitkala-sa, Red Bird,
truly spread her wings in flight.

Jim Thorpe

(Sac and Fox) 1887–1953

Jim Thorpe's Indian name
was Wathahuck,
the Light After the Lightning.

And Jim was almost
as fast as lightning.
No one could jump higher,
no one was stronger,
or more determined than Jim.

He said it was
because of his twin brother,
Charlie, who died of a fever
when the two were very young.
Jim said Charlie's strength
was given to him.

Jim never wanted
to go to school.
He wanted to stay
home with his family,
hunt and fish, and roam
the hills of Indian territory.

But his father insisted,
and even though he ran away
time after time
to come back home,
his father always
sent him back again.

Until at last his father
decided to send him
to a school where
it would be hard
to run away.
"Son," he said,
"it is time for you
to prove what
an Indian can do."

So it was that
Jim ended up
in Pennsylvania at
the Carlisle Indian School.

It was there that he found
his purpose in life,
for Carlisle was known
for its great teams,
and playing games
was something Jim
had always loved.

He proved to Pop Warner,
the track and field coach,
that he could jump higher
than anyone on his team
and soon became a star.

But when he asked
to play football,
at first Pop Warner
told him no,
for Jim was still
not that big then
and Pop didn't want
his best trackman hurt.

Then Jim took the football
and ran the length of the field
and back and even though
everyone tried to tackle him,
no one could bring him down.

It didn't matter what it was,
football or baseball
or track and field,
Jim always was the best,
never bragging,
always modest.

So it was that
in 1918 he was sent
to the Olympics in Sweden
where no one yet
knew who he was
until he won not just one
but two gold medals
for the pentathlon
and the decathlon.

That was when
the king of Sweden said,
as he placed a laurel wreath
on Jim's head,
"Sir, you are the greatest
athlete in the world."
"Thanks, King," is what
Jim replied to him.

Jim went on to
play pro sports,
baseball and football,
where he became
the head of what
would one day become
the National Football League.

He worked in Hollywood,
toured the country
giving lectures, the best-known
and best-loved Native American
of his time with a movie made
about his life.

That great fame never
went to Jim's head.
If anyone ever needed help,
they could always count
on a hand from Jim,
a man who had done
as his father asked
and truly shown the world
what an Indian could do.

Gladys Tantaquidgeon

(Mohegan) 1899–2005

The women elders
selected her at the age of five
to learn the traditions of her
Mohegan people,
including the ways
of the Makiawisug,
the little people
who guard the medicines.

She never forgot
any of that teaching,
even after she left Mohegan Hill
for the University of Pennsylvania
where she studied anthropology
and after her graduation
was hired by the Bureau of Indian Affairs
and sent to South Dakota
to administer social service benefits
on the Yankton Indian reservation.

Her job soon changed
when she was transferred
to the Indian Arts and Crafts Board
where her job was to help
Native artists keep and develop
their traditional arts and skills.
But also while she was there
she encouraged them
to restore those traditional ways
that would strengthen
the heart of their nation,
such as ceremonies the government
had prohibited,
like the sacred Sun Dance.

After 13 years of doing this work,
she returned home to Mohegan Hill,
to the Tantaquidgeon Indian Museum
founded by her and her family,
to work full-time there
for the next half century
encouraging the preservation
and revival of
their language and customs,
always remembering
whenever she ate
to always first offer
a bit of her food
to the Makiawisug.

Not only did she become
the Medicine Woman of her people,
and a strong voice on
their tribal council,
all of the records
and documents
she had kept for decades
under her bed
were used in the Mohegan tribe's
case for federal recognition,
which was granted to them in 1994.

When her feet at last
found the road of stars
at the age of 106,
she left behind
a nation made strong
by her words and her work
that began when
a little girl of five
was taught to listen
to the little people,
the guardians of healing.

Left:
Jeffrey Gibson
Mississippi Band Choctaw/Cherokee
This is Our House, 2014

Artwork © Jeffrey Gibson,
courtesy of Sikkema Jenkins & Co., New York;
KaviGupta Gallery, Chicago;
Regen Projects, Los Angeles;
Stephen Friedman Gallery, London
Photo: Pete Mauney

Right:
Andy Everson
K'omoks and Kwakwa̱ka'wakw
Resistance
Image and photo: Courtesy of the artist

Elizabeth Wanamaker Peratrovich

(Tlingit) 1911–1958

Elizabeth was adopted
as a baby.
In those years when
tuberculosis
affected so many
Alaskan Native
communities,
children often
found themselves
with new parents.
Luckily for her,
those who took her in
as their daughter
were a Tlingit family,
the Wanamakers,
who raised her in Ketchikan.
They spoke English and
their Tlingit language
and reminded her
of her place
as a member of the
Raven moiety of the proud
Lukaax.adi Tlingit Clan.

And despite the
way she was told
in school to speak
only English,
punished by being forced
to kneel on sharp stones
for saying even
one Tlingit word,
she never forgot
her proud heritage.

After going to college
in the state of Washington
and marrying her husband
Roy, also a Tlingit,
the two of them returned
with their children
to Juneau, where
they discovered that
things hadn't changed
since when she was a child.
It was as bad
for Alaska Natives
as it was for
Blacks in the South.
Elizabeth did not give up.

She soon became
the president of the
Alaska Native Sisterhood.
She and her husband
began to lobby
the territory's legislators
to pass an act
of anti-discrimination.

It soon became clear
to everyone that Elizabeth's voice
was the strongest of them all,
as powerful as a Raven's call.

At last in 1945,
the Alaskan Senate
gathered to vote
on the bill to grant
Natives equal rights.
There was bitter opposition.

One senator said,
"Who are these people
barely out of savagery
to associate with us whites
with 5,000 years
of recorded civilization behind us?"

Elizabeth was last to testify.
Her speech was an impassioned one.
It swayed more than one mind
as she spoke of how
she and her children
had to endure
a second-class existence,
unable to live
in a good neighborhood,
refused entrance into movies,
seeing signs in shop windows
that read
No Dogs or Natives allowed.

"I would not have expected,"
she said to the Senate,
"that I, barely out of savagery,
would have to remind gentlemen
with 5,000 years of recorded
civilization behind them,
of the Bill of Rights."

The bill was passed 11–5,
signed into law nearly 20 years
before the United States Congress
passed the Civil Rights Act of 1964.

Elizabeth Peratrovich
became known
as the fighter in velvet gloves,
a leader in the fight
for all human rights.

Zoë Urness
Tlingit
Hopi Maiden
Image and photo: Courtesy of the artist

Maria Tallchief

(Osage) 1925–2013

She came from
the red earth of Oklahoma,
that land her people
tried hard to defend.

Others wanted
what the Osages had—
not just the soil
but the wealth of black oil
that lay beneath it,
a blessing and a curse.

But what Maria wanted
was never wealth.
She wanted to express herself
in that old way her people
had always known
through the motion of dance.

Just as her ancestors
found the bear in their songs,
she too felt all of nature
as she moved.

She longed to spin
like a leaf in the wind,
to leap with the grace
of the deer. And when,
after long years of practice—
which made her feet ache
and every limb of her body
feel at times as heavy as stone—
she took the main stage
and it was clear that
no one could dance like her.

She was the first
to flame as the Firebird,
a phoenix rising,
her feet carrying her
far beyond Oklahoma,
leaping across oceans
and spinning back again,
thrilling thousands.
And when her own days
of performance were done,
she opened her heart
to nurture a new generation.

She was not only
the first Native woman
to star in a ballet,
the first American prima ballerina,
but one who remembered
that those who find
a new trail must not forget
to guide those who follow.

Steven Paul Judd
Kiowa and Choctaw
Space Invaders
Image and photo: Courtesy of the artist

Chester Nez

(Diné) 1921–2014

As a young boy
he was sent to the boarding school.
There, far away from
his family hogan
and the sheep and goats
he cared for with such love,
he was told
to forget his sacred language
and all things
that made him Navajo.
His long hair
was sheared off
and he was taught
the English language
and how to pray
in the Catholic way.

Such praying was good,
but so, too, were the prayers
he still spoke in Diné.

When the Second World War
began for America,
they volunteered
to fight for Namaha,
their motherland.
Even though his people
had been badly treated
in the past, his entire nation
during the time of the Civil War
driven from their homes,
sent on the Long Walk
to a prisoner of war camp
in barren lands to the east,
for years before being
allowed to return,
even though, within
his own lifetime,
misguided government policies
had decreed the slaughter
of nearly all of their sheep,
their goats, and their horses,
still he and many other Diné men
volunteered to serve in
the American army.
As much as any other man,
this land was theirs
to love and defend,
as much as any other man's.

Chester's job in that war
was a different one.
Recruited with 28 other Navajos,
boarding school graduates
who spoke good English,
they were given a special mission—
to use their language,
a tongue that no one
but Navajos could speak,
to create a secret unbreakable code.

Every other American code
had been broken by their enemies
in the wide Pacific
theater of war.

But the Navajo code
that they created
was never deciphered.
Not only did they
use Diné code words,
such as a-ye-shi "egg" in Navajo
when they spoke of bombs,
they also spelled out
messages, with a Diné term
for each letter of the alphabet
such as Wolachee for Ant
and Shush for Bear.

It worked so well
that soon more than
400 other Navajo men
worked as Code Talkers,
part of every operation
throughout the whole Pacific,
from Guadalcanal
to Okinawa.

It was never easy,
carrying a gun and a radio,
facing death day after day.
But Chester never faltered
and he returned home,
just before the war's end.
But the battles he'd fought
and the enemies' faces
played like an endless
film reel in his dreams.
It was not until

his family arranged
a special traditional sing—
a four day long
Enemy Way ceremony
done to free
his mind, his body,
and his spirit
from the darkness of war—
that he again found
balance and peace.

So secret was
the work he did,
that he could tell no one
about being a Code Talker
until decades later.

Then, at last, he and
those surviving men
who all had been taught
in boarding schools
to forget everything
about their culture
and then were asked
to use the sacred language
they'd been forbidden to speak
to help America,
were honored, given medals,
invited to the White House.

With the help of a friend
in his final years,
when he was the last
of those first 29 men,
he wrote a book about
his own life.

"Our story," he wrote
on that book's final page,
"is not one of sorrow,
like the Long Walk
and the Great Livestock Massacre,
but one of triumph."

Wilma Mankiller

(Cherokee) 1945–2010

Wilma Mankiller,
whose Aniyunwiya name
was A-ji-lusghi, The Flower,
was no delicate blossom,
but always a fighter.
Her life honored
the Mankiller name,
that in the language
of her people
was Asgaya-dihi,
denoting one
who was a leader
in battle or one
with the power
to avenge wrongs.

Not only did she fight
the battles a chief
must engage in
for her nation,
she fought back
from the car accident
that almost took her life
and would have crippled
not just the body
but the spirit of one
whose determination
was less than hers.

And when illness
after illness
came, she did not
give in but continued
to speak and act
for her people and
for the rights of
all Native women
who took courage
from her example.

Chemotherapy,
kidney transplants,
sexism even
within her own nation,
everything that might
have kept another
from pushing on,
did not deter her.

From an Oklahoma
childhood so poor that
her mother
made the clothes for her
and her sisters and brothers
from feed sacks,
to the takeover
of Alcatraz Island,
to her own struggle
to gain an education
that she could use
to build a new way
of self-determination
for her tribe and for all
the other nations,
she never faltered.

First, succeeding
against great odds
in bringing water
to their dry lands,
then rising to become
the first woman
to be elected
as the Head Chief
of the Cherokee Nation,
bringing back into
their tribal rolls,
thousands who once
had been forgotten.

The role she played
as a unifier, a true
peacemaker, one unafraid
to always speak up
when others were silent
was so much like
that past warrior
known as Nancy Ward
that it would be
no exaggeration to say
that she became her people's
Beloved Woman.

Rory Wakemup
Boise Forte Band of the Minnesota Chippewa
Neon Chief
Image and photo: Courtesy of the artist

Above:
Sonny Assu
Ligwiłda'xw of the Kwakwa̱ka̱'wakw Nations
Skeena, Beam Me Up!, 2015
Image and photo: Courtesy of the artist and
Equinox Gallery (Vancouver) and Art Mur (Montreal)

Right:
Norman Akers
Osage Nation
Internalized Stories, 2018
Image: Courtesy of the artist
Photo: Brian Hawkins

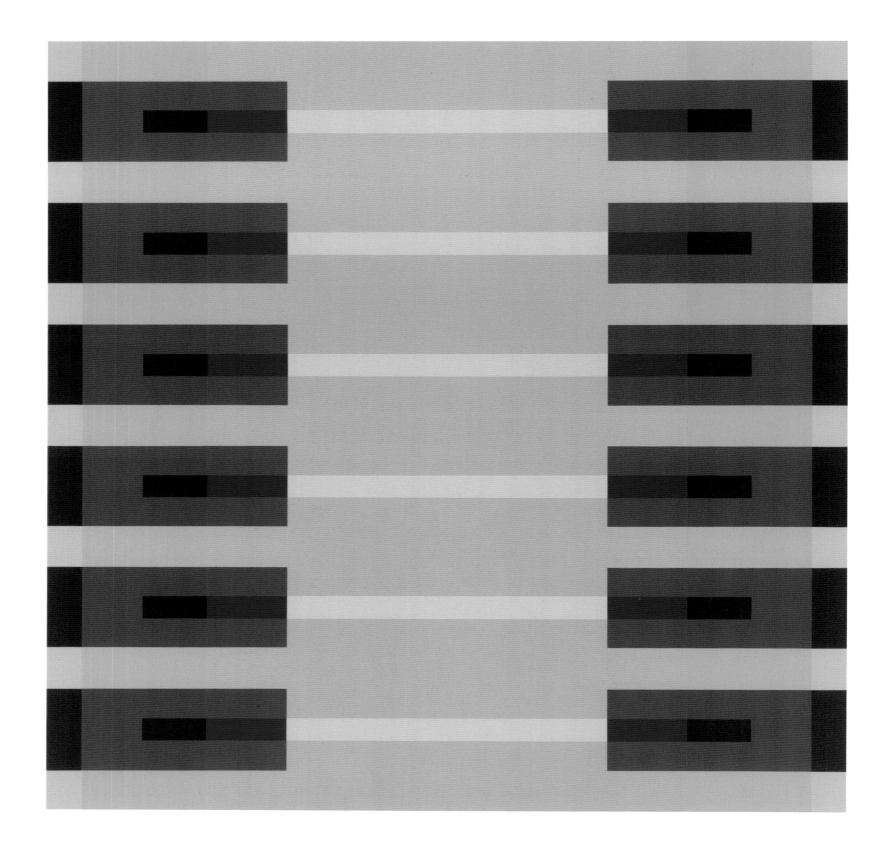

Jordan Ann Craig

Northern Cheyenne

Are We Going To Kiss

Image: Courtesy of the artist
Photo: Tonee Harbert

MORE ABOUT THE VOICES

The Peacemaker

The Haudenosaunee are five tribal nations speaking a common language (with several dialects). Today those nations are best known by the names of Mohawk, Oneida, Onondaga, Cayuga, and Seneca. Their original homelands included much of contemporary New York State. Despite their common culture, the Five Nations were engaged in bitter warfare at the time of the Peacemaker, perhaps 1,000 years ago. Their representative form of government, created by the Peacemaker and his allies, influenced such founding fathers of the United States as Benjamin Franklin in the creation of the American Constitution.

Jikonsahseh

Jikonsahseh's role in founding the Great League of Peace is echoed in the structure of Haudenosaunee culture to this day. The clan mothers chose the men from their nation who would be among the 50 representatives of their community at the meetings of the Great League at Onondaga. Also, if any of those men behaved badly, the women of his clan could "dehorn" him. They could remove him from office and symbolically take away the deer horns that stood for his role as a leader—one who speaks for his people and not for himself.

Malintzin/La Malinche

The most common image of the Spanish Conquest of Mexico is that of conquistadors on horseback doing it all by themselves. But the powerful Aztec empire could never have been defeated without the aid of thousands of Native allies. Again and again over the next four centuries, Europeans would use Native allies who were traditional enemies of whatever indigenous nation they were fighting. Malintzin's alliance with Cortés is the first recorded example of that. Her controversial story also points out, for better or worse, the power of indigenous women.

Pocahontas

The Powhatan Confederacy included a number of tribal nations in the coastal areas of contemporary Maryland and northern Virginia. The head of the confederacy was called the Powhatan. It is estimated that as many as 20,000 people were part of the powerful alliance when the English established their colony of Jamestown, the first English attempt at colonization in North America. Among the contemporary Virginia Native nations who were part of that alliance are the Chickahominy, the Mattaponi, and the Nansemond.

As the daughter of the head of the Powhatan, Pocahontas was a crucial figure in the early years of the colony, first as a go-between committed to peace, then as a hostage, and finally as the wife of colonist John Rolfe.

Tisquantum

Plimoth Plantation was the first successful English Colony due in large part to the Pautuxet man known as Tisquantum, or Squanto. He spoke English because he had been taken by force from his Native land and sold into slavery in Europe. Freed from slavery, he returned to North America and found that his people were gone—the victims of some disease brought accidentally by European traders. Tisquantum decided to assist the English colonists who had chosen the site of his abandoned village for their settlement. He taught them the survival skills, including how to grow corn, beans, and squash, that they needed. He also was the main translator between the English and the nearby Wampanoags.

Po'pay

The Pueblos are a number of different tribal nations who have long lived in villages throughout the Rio Grande valley in present-day New Mexico. They were named "Pueblos" by the Spanish because they lived in multi-story adobe buildings. They were harshly treated by the Spanish who established colonies there in the late 16th century. At the time of Spanish arrival, there were over 110 separate pueblos with a combined population of more than 80,000 people. By 1680, only 40 pueblos remained and the population was no more than 17,000. So there was good reason for their uprising. Po'pay's was the first and most successful rebellion by Native Americans against European invaders. It took 12 years for the Spanish to return and regain control.

Kateri Tekakwitha

In many Native American communities, Christianity was introduced as early as the 16th century. Native people often saw great similarity between their beliefs in the Great Mystery and the new religion being brought by such missionaries as the French Jesuits. In many contemporary Native American communities, Christianity is quite central. The Kateri Tekakwitha National Shrine and Historic Site is in Fonda, New York near the place where she was born.

Pontiac/Obwandiyag

The homelands of the Odawa, or Ottawa, whose name is said to mean "Traders," were in parts of present-day Michigan, Ontario (Canada), Wisconsin, and northern Iowa. They were well known for their diplomatic skills. As American colonization pushed west, many Native nations were being pushed off their own land. The Odawa had been allies of the French who were engaged in a war with the British over the control of the continent. That war ended in 1763 with the Treaty of Paris and the French withdrawal back into Canada. Without their European allies, the tribal nations were on their own against the British. The scene was set for them to come together and resist. Although Pontiac's alliance failed, it did result in the 1766 proclamation that the land west of the mountains would forever be Indian land. One of the reasons for the American Revolution was the desire of the American colonies to take the Native land protected by the British agreement of 1766. In the century that followed the American Revolution, many of the Odawas were pushed west from Ohio to Kansas and then Oklahoma where the contemporary Ottawa Tribe of Oklahoma now exists.

Samson Occum

Samson Occum was only one of many Native Americans who gained a higher education in the mid-18th century and chose to enter the clergy. His Mohegan people, who still live on their traditional lands in Connecticut, saw the value of western education early on. An educated Indian could serve as a bridge between cultures—as Occum attempted to do. As a preacher, Occum was able to speak for Indians in general, work among his own people, and try to provide for their welfare.

Ganio-Dai-Yo/Handsome Lake

Visionary experience is a central part of the cultures of many different tribal nations. The idea of someone becoming a messenger from the Creator is accepted. Although not all of the people of the Five Nations accepted Handsome Lake's message as an authentic one, many saw him as the next in line of a series of such heaven-inspired messengers as the Peacemaker. Rather than preaching resistance to the whites, Handsome Lake's teachings stressed a return to family values and certain traditional ways while accepting such aspects of the majority culture as keeping livestock. However, he was deeply opposed to Christianity, which he saw as a destructive force. In the troubled time after the American Revolution, his Good Message brought hope to his Seneca people and many others in the Iroquois League. Today about 10,000 Seneca people live in New York State, where the Seneca Nation of New York and the Tonawanda Reservation still exist in their traditional lands while approximately 1,000 other Senecas live on the Six Nations Reserve in Ontario (Canada).

Nancy Ward/Nanyehi

Women have always played a central role among the Aniyunwiya, the Principal People, as the Cherokee call themselves. They are the owners of the homes, heads of the families, and a person's clan is inherited from the mother. The Beloved Woman was the one whose voice carried perhaps the most weight in every council meeting. In the late 18th century, the Cherokee adopted so many aspects of European American culture that they became known as one of the Five Civilized Tribes. Despite this and the efforts of people such as Nancy Ward to maintain peace with their white neighbors, in the early 19th century they were forced to leave their homelands in Georgia, the Carolinas, and Tennessee and travel on the Trail of Tears to Indian Territory. Today the Cherokee have two main population centers—in Oklahoma and in North Carolina. Currently, their total tribal enrollment is over 380,000 worldwide with over 140,000 residing in Oklahoma and 13,000 enrolled Eastern Cherokee members in North Carolina.

Sacajawea

The traditional lands of Sacajawea's people, Eastern Shoshone people, are in Wyoming on the eastern side of the Rocky Mountains. The Lewis and Clark expedition valued Sacajawea's presence at first because they thought she could help them get horses from her people, horses needed to cross those mountains. However, they soon began to value her for her intelligence and her warm personality. She turned out to be one of the main reasons for their success and was treated almost as a daughter by Clark who called her "Janey" and later welcomed her into his home and provided an education for her children. Today, the eastern Shoshone share their more than two million acre Wind River Reservation in Wyoming with the Northern Arapahos. It is at Wind River where tribal historians say Sacajawea lived out the rest of her long life and where her grave can be found.

Sequoyah

Sequoyah is the first person in recorded history known to have created a writing system for an entire language. Further, he was illiterate—unable to read or write any other language—before starting work on his system. Although he used signs that drew on both traditional motifs and letters in the English alphabet, each of the characters in his script stood for a syllable or sound in his language. The total number of characters in his syllabary ended up at 85. His system was so accurate and so easy to learn that a Cherokee speaker could begin to read and write it in a short time. The syllabary is still used to this day by the Cherokee Nation.

Jeffrey Gibson
Mississippi Band Choctaw/Cherokee
I'm Gonna Try Just a Little Bit Harder, 2015
Artwork © Jeffrey Gibson, courtesy of Sikkema Jenkins & Co., New York;
KaviGupta Gallery, Chicago; Regen Projects, Los Angeles;
Stephen Friedman Gallery, London
Photo: Pete Mauney

Ely Parker Donehogawa

Ely S. Parker was born at a time in the 19th century when his Seneca nation faced the loss of what little land was left to it. Land companies were eager to take the small Tonawanda reservation where he lived. He was chosen by the elders to become a defender of his people by gaining an education. He exceeded their expectations. By the time he was in his late teens he was more fluent as a writer and speaker of English than most white men, respected for his eloquence as an orator. He met, and was in most cases on friendly terms, with every president of the United States from Polk to Lincoln and served in the administration of Grant. He was a major factor in helping the Tonawandas save their reservation and was elevated to being a royaner or "chief" at the age of 23 with the new name of Do-ne-ho-ga-wa. Few Native Americans managed to bridge the gap between the white and Native worlds as successfully as he did.

Geronimo/Goyathlay

The Chiricahua Apaches originally lived in parts of present-day Arizona and Mexico. Their name for themselves, Inday, means "the people." Apache means "enemy" in one of the nearby Pueblo languages. Chiricahua probably comes from the name for the wild turkeys, so common on their homelands. Their primary enemies at the time when Americans took over the southwest, were the Mexicans, who had a history of killing and enslaving Apaches. Virtually every Chiricahua family had at least one relative who had been captured and enslaved in Mexico. Geronimo's first wife and children were killed by Mexicans when he was a young man. Apache attempts to live in peace with the Americans failed and their resistance—in which Geronimo was a central figure—led to his legendary long decades of resistance. His final surrender marked the end of the centuries' long "Indian Wars" of the United States with Native tribal nations. After decades of exile in a prison camp in Alabama, he was allowed to go with the rest of his people to Oklahoma where he lived out his remaining years at Fort Sill.

Standing Bear/Ma-Chu-Na-Zhe

The Osage, who call themselves Wazhaze, "the mid-waters people," originated in the Ohio and Mississippi River valleys and migrated west after the 17th century as a result of the Iroquois invading the Ohio Valley. They were sometimes described as the tallest and best-looking people in North America. Some Osage men were as much as 7 feet tall. In the 19th century they were forced to remove from Kansas to Oklahoma. Early in the 20th century oil was discovered on their land and many of them became wealthy. However, during the early 20th century, many Osage people were defrauded and even murdered by white men to take over their wealth. Originally a part of the Omaha tribe, in the early 18th century they migrated west from the Great Lakes region, settling in Nebraska and South Dakota. They never went to war with the United States and signed their first peace treaty with the US in 1817. Even so, they were relocated by the US government to Indian territory in 1877 where about a third of their people died, including the oldest son of Standing Bear.

Sitting Bull/Ttanka Iyotake

When most non-Natives think of American Indians the image that comes into their heads is of people living in tipis, hunting buffalo on horseback, and wearing eagle feather headdresses. That image, stereotyped as it may be, comes from the Lakota people—the nation from which Sitting Bull came. There are 7 Fires or tribal divisions among the Lakota. His own nation was the Hunkpapa, whose homelands include the area now known as Nebraska, North Dakota, and South Dakota where their present-day reservations are located. Hunkpapa means "Head of the Circle."

Crazy Horse/Tashunka Witco

The tradition of being made invulnerable to firearms by either medicine or a spiritual gift was found widely among the various nations of the Great Plains. Crazy Horse is perhaps the best-known example of a warrior who was never struck in battle by a bullet. He never allowed his photo to be taken and there are no authenticated pictures of him. Today over 28,000 Oglala people live on the Pine Ridge Reservation in South Dakota. It's the site of both the massacre of Lakota people at Wounded Knee and the armed standoff at Wounded Knee in 1973 when Native activists were besieged by government forces for 71 days. The residents of Pine Ridge have one of the lowest life expectancies in America and are the poorest reservation community in the United States. However, Pine Ridge is also the site of the Oglala Lakota College, founded in 1971 and there are determined efforts on the part of many in its community to better the lives of their people—"In the Spirit of Crazy Horse."

Buffalo Calf Road Woman

The Cheyenne, whose name comes from Lakota and means something like "Allies" call themselves Tsitsistas, which translates to "those like us" or "human beings." Like the Lakotas, their original lands were in the Midwest and they migrated to the western plains where they reinvented their way of life as buffalo hunters, engaging in the great game practiced by all the Plains people of raiding other nations for horses and proving their bravery by "counting coup"—touching the enemy in battle. Never a large nation in numbers, they were formidable fighters and, with their allies the Arapaho, controlled trading in the central plains. They also often allied with the Lakotas, camping with them and joining them in war. Held in captivity after Custer's defeat, in 1878 a group of 300 Cheyenne people–including Buffalo Calf Road Woman—broke out of the reservation at Fort Reno and tried to make their way back north in an epic journey that inspired the novel *Cheyenne Autumn*. Today the Cheyenne can be found in two communities, the Northern Cheyenne Reservation in Montana and the Cheyenne and Arapaho Nation in Oklahoma.

Robert I. Mesa
Navajo of the Navajo Nation and
Soboba part of the Band of Mission Indians
brothers or flight
Image and photo: Courtesy of the artist

Quanah Parker

Confined now to a reservation in Oklahoma, the original territory of the Comanche people stretched throughout the southern plains including much of what is now known as southwestern Kansas, eastern New Mexico, southeastern Colorado, western Oklahoma, and northern Texas. Their name for themselves which means "the people" is Numuunu, often called "the Lords of the Plains." The horse became a key element in their culture, giving them a great advantage in times of war. Originally part of the Shoshone tribe to the north they moved onto the plains in the 17th century.

Their practice of adopting captures, so common to many Native nations, was what resulted in Quanah Parker's mother becoming part of the people and never wanting to leave them.

Chief Joseph/In-Mut-Too-Yah-Lat-Lat

The Nez Perce call themselves Nimiipuu, which means "The People." The name Nez Perce, which means "pierced nose" (although the Nimiipuu have never pierced their noses), was given them by French fur traders. Known for their ability as horse breeders, the durable, strong, and agile Appaloosa horse was developed by them and used in their famous retreat while pursued by several American armies. It's estimated that they lived in the same area of the northwestern plateau on the eastern slope of the Rocky Mountains for 10,000 years or more. Today their reservation in north central Idaho is located on part of the land that was their traditional territory.

Lozen

Although Lozen was the most famous Chiricahua warrior woman, it was not uncommon for Apache women to accompany their husbands on raids and women with special gifts as fighters sometimes became warriors. All of the Chiricahua people were sent as prisoners of war to Florida and Alabama and Oklahoma at the end of the 19th century. In a photograph taken of the Chiricahua prisoners of war alongside the rail tracks partway through their long journey into exile, Lozen can be clearly seen. She died while a POW in Mount Vernon from tuberculosis, which killed many of the Chiricahuas during those years in captivity. Today most Chiricahua Apache live on their reservation in the area of Fort Sill, Oklahoma.

Sarah Winnemucca/Thocmetony

The homeland of the Northern Paiute people, who call themselves Numa, ("The People"), was originally in the area of eastern California, western Nevada, and southeast Oregon. Divided into many bands, each associated with a certain place, such as the Pyramid Lake area where Sarah's people lived. They were known as the Kuyuidika-a Paiute because one of their primary foods was the cui-uwi (kwee-wee) fish of Pyramid Lake. Between the Pyramid Lake War in1860 and the Bannock War of 1878, a number of violent confrontations with European Americans took place as more of their lands were claimed by white settlers. Smallpox and other infectious diseases for which they had no resistance also swept through the Northern Paiutes at this time.

Sarah's 1883 book *Life Among the Piutes* gives a first-hand account of this period.

Today, there are a number of different Paiute reservations in several western states. The reservation of Sarah Winnemucca's Pyramid Lake Paiute Tribe is located on 475,000 acres near Reno, Nevada.

Wovoka

Wovoka's band of Northern Paiutes lived in the area of the Walker Valley of central Nevada where their current reservation is located. His people represented two bands, the Aga-idokado, the Cutthroat Trout Easters, and the Pakwisokado, the Chub Carp Eaters. Wovoka's own name means "Cutter" or "Wood Cutter." It was common for Paiute men during his time to work as he did as a farmhand for nearby white ranchers. Cattle grazing is the most common use of their lands today.

His vision of the Ghost Dance came to him after a solar eclipse in 1889. Those who lived righteously and danced in a circle holding hands would be given a land of love and peace.

Although the Ghost Dance he created swept across tribal nations of the west, the last part of his life was quiet after the initial fervor of his prophetic movement ended following the tragic events at Wounded Knee. Wovoka was buried four decades after the failure of his vision on the Walker Valley Reservation in the town of Shurz.

Charles Alexander Eastman/Ohiyesa

The Santee Sioux reservation in Nebraska was established in 1863. This was after the "Great Minnesota Sioux Uprising" in their original homelands, which was sparked by mistreatment and broken government promises. At the end of the conflict a military tribunal sentenced more than 300 Santee men to death. Most of their lives were spared when President Lincoln commuted their sentences. However, the 38 men named as ringleaders were hanged in the largest mass execution in US history in 1862 in Mankato, Minnesota.

Born in a buffalo hide tipi near Redwood Falls, Minnesota, Charles Alexander Eastman or Ohiyesa ("The Winner") went on to be educated at Dartmouth and Boston College. He then worked as a physician on several reservations in South Dakota before becoming active in Native rights. Among his accomplishments were the founding of dozens of Native American chapters of the YMCA, helping found the Boy Scouts of America, and becoming the most prolific and respected Native author of his time.

Susan La Flesche

The homeland of the Omaha (Upstream People) is in the Midwest, where the Omaha Reservation still exists in northeastern Nebraska and western Iowa. Susan La Flesche's father Joseph Insta Maza (Iron Eye) La Flesche was the last traditional chief of the Omaha nation and also of Ponca descent. Susan and her four siblings were raised with Omaha as their first language and they were all as outstanding and accomplished as Susan was. Most notably, her sister Susette was a teacher, journalist, and writer who provided crucial help to Standing Bear in his battle for basic rights for Native Americans and Susan's half-brother Francis was an ethnologist for the Smithsonian Institution who wrote important books about the Omaha and Osage nations.

Elizabeth Burton "Lyda" Conley

The Wyandot people originated from the St. Lawrence area of Quebec, Canada where they were called Huron by the French and where the Huron/Wendat nation still exists. However, pushed west by the Iroquois, many Wyandot settled in Ohio and Michigan before being forced to Kansas and then Oklahoma. As a result there are today four recognized Wendat, Wyandot, and Wyandotte nations in different parts of the continent. Lyda's own Wyandot nation of Kansas eventually gained state recognition and, in 1998, the Wyandottes of Oklahoma agreed with them to preserve the Huron Cemetery in Kansas City for religious and cultural use.

Gertrude Simmons/Zitkala-Sa

There are three main divisions of the people called the Sioux—the Lakotas, the Eastern Dakotas, and the Yankton Western Dakotas, who call themselves Ihanktonwan Dakota Oyate—"People of the End Village." All three of these divisions originally lived in the Midwest on the upper Mississippi but were forced west onto the Great Plains by the Anishinabe and their French allies.

On the Great Plains, they developed a new culture dependent upon the horse and buffalo hunting. The current home of the Yankton people, since 1859, is a nearly 475,000-acre reservation in South Dakota.

Zitkala-Sa was celebrated in her early career as a musician and a writer. After attending a government boarding school, she went on to Earlham College. Published in the *Atlantic Monthly,* and then authoring two highly praised books, her work became known to the wider American public in the early decades of the 20th century. She then moved on to focus her efforts on Native rights. In 1926, she was the co-founder of the National Council of American Indians and served as its president until her death in 1938 in Washington DC, where her last resting place is the Arlington National Cemetery.

Jim Thorpe

The Sac and Fox nation of Oklahoma originated from the area of Iowa. The name Sac or Sauk comes from their name for themselves, Thakiwaki, or "People Coming Forth from the Water." "Fox" was actually the name of one of the clans of the Meskwaki people who still reside in Iowa. Forced from their lands after the Black Hawk War in 1832, the Sac and Fox eventually reestablished themselves—as did dozens of other tribal groups—in the Indian Territory that became Oklahoma. Those relocated Native nations, including the Sac and Fox, had their reservation terminated in a series of people claims to 160 acres of "free" land each. Native people were also allocated acreage, but lost most of the land that had been theirs. However, the Sac and Fox stayed on what land was left. Today their tribal headquarters are on former reservation lands near Stroud, Oklahoma where most of their people still live. Jim's son Jack Thorpe was influential in getting back some of the land lost by their people when Jack was chief of their nation.

Jim Thorpe's athletic ability may have been inherited from his father. Hiram Thorpe was celebrated for being able to beat anyone in foot races and all sorts of contests, though his fame never went beyond their tribal nation.

Gladys Tantaquidgeon

The Mohegan people are a northeastern tribal nation whose name means Wolf People. James Fenimore Cooper's novel *The Last of the Mohicans* used the names of real Mohegan leaders, such as Uncas, but did not tell a story connected to the Mohegans. Unlike many northeastern Native nations, they avoided removal and remained in the area around Mohegan Hull in Uncasville, Connecticut. They were finally acknowledged as a surviving tribal nation with federal recognition in 1994. Gladys Tantaquidgeon's niece Melissa Tantaquidgeon Zobel is a well-known author who published a biography of her aunt entitled *Medicine Trail, the Life and Lessons of Gladys Tantaquidgeon.*

Elizabeth Wanamaker Peratrovich

Southeast Alaska is the homeland of the Tlingit people, whose name means "People of the Tides." Known for their ability as woodcarvers and woodworkers—creating huge long houses and canoes and giant totem poles—much of their way of life remains dependent upon the sea and salmon is one of their main food staples. Russian surnames and membership in the Russian Orthodox church reflects their early contact in the 17th century with Russian traders and priests. Fierce offenders of their homeland, they resisted the Russians in the 1802 and 1804 battles of Sitka.

In 2020, when a new dollar coin was released by the United States mint, Elizabeth's image and her name were stamped upon it.

Maria Tallchief

The Osage nation originated in the Ohio Valley but migrated west in the 17th century under pressure from the Iroquois to find new hunting grounds in Kansas. Described by writers of the time as the tallest and best-looking of the American Indian nations, many Osage men were well over 6 feet and sometimes 7 feet tall. Forced by the government to move again in the 19th century, they managed to keep the mineral rights to the land in Indian Territory where they were sent. This was both lucky and unlucky for them when large deposits of oil were found on their reservation. While many became wealthy, many other Osage people were swindled or even murdered for their oil money.

Today the Osage nation still exists in Oklahoma. Their tribal headquarters are in Pawhuska, Oklahoma and they are the only federally recognized tribe in the state to have kept their lands as a reservation.

Dance is a part of virtually every Native American culture. However, the idea of a Native woman becoming a ballerina, much less perhaps the most famous prima ballerina in the world, was unthinkable when Maria Tallchief started studying ballet.

Chester Nez

No one is quite sure how many Navajo men served as code talkers during World War II, but the number was well over 400. The reason for that uncertainty is that their role was top secret, a secret officially kept until decades after the end of World War II. The names of the first 29, however, are now well known. Chester and the other 28 men in that group, all fluent in both English and Navajo, created that unbreakable code on their own using the Navajo language. It was so effective that it became the primary means to send coded messages throughout the last years of the war against the Japanese forces throughout the entire Pacific region. Chester's autobiography, *Code Talker,* and Samuel Holiday's *Under The Eagle* are the only two books about the code talkers written by code talkers themselves.

Wilma Mankiller

Wilma Mankiller's Oklahoma Cherokee nation was deeply impacted by her time working for them and as their Principal Chief from 1985 to 1995. Their land base was small, their rate of poverty high, and there were many Cherokees who lacked even drinkable water. A movie was made based on her work—even before she became chief—to bring water to their community: *The Cherokee Name for Water.* Few people overcame as many obstacles as Wilma did, before, during, and after her terms in office. They included a near-fatal car accident which required plastic surgery to reconstruct her face, chemotherapy for cancer, and two kidney transplants. But she continued to work as a voice for her people, as a crusader for Native rights, and a person concerned with women's issues throughout the world all throughout her inspiring life.

Cannupa Hanska Luger
Enrolled member of the Three Affiliated Tribes of Fort Berthold and is of Mandan, Hidatsa, Arikara, and Lakota descent
This Is Not A Snake/The One Who Checks & The One Who Balances 2017–2020

Image: Courtesy of the artist
Photo: Craig Smith for Heard Museum, 2020

ABOUT THE AUTHOR

My journey began
with my grandfather's hands,
digging into the good earth
his hands as brown as the soil.

He never told me
the stories of our ancestry,
yet I know now that
the way he taught me
to love the soil,
to listen to the birds,
and be grateful for
each day
were gifts as simple and clear
as the water of
a roadside spring,
gifts that would
help me grow.

There in my grandparents' care,
our home was far enough
removed from town
that my best friends
were not people,
but books and the trees
of the forest that would
one day become
a nature preserve
cared for by my own sons.

Aside from saying
that he left school
in the fourth grade
because they kept
calling him a dirty Indian
my grandfather, Jesse Bowman,
spoke little of his heritage.

Somehow, it made me
more determined to know
the stories he never told,
to seek out elders,
relatives I'd never met,
keepers of truths
that I listened to,
cherishing every word
they shared.

Then I went on
to tell those stories
to my own two sons
so that they would know
the roots I only
began to uncover,
and trace in my late teens.

That path of stories
that held my feet
then led me on,
not just into
the shadowed
past of my own family
but beyond to those
of other nations who,
like our Abenaki people
had been made invisible,
erased, or set aside.

So, though you may
be reading my words,
though you may be
hearing me speak,
remember that for
every page I've written,
for every story I've told
there are countless voices
stronger than my own.
Remember that I am
and will always be
one who listens
more than he speaks,
grateful to those elders
who were kind enough,
generous enough,
strong enough
to share and keep sharing.

One of the maples
my grandfather and I
planted long ago
towers over this house
where I was raised.

And now as I
dig my own fingers
into this good earth
that holds our stories
my hope is that
whatever I plant
will grow well
for our children's children.